The Role of the Public Sector
Economics and Society

Bent Greve

Professor in Social Science, Department of Social Sciences and Business, University of Roskilde, Denmark

Edward Elgar
PUBLISHING

Cheltenham, UK • Northampton, MA, USA

Published by
Edward Elgar Publishing Limited
The Lypiatts
15 Lansdown Road
Cheltenham
Glos GL50 2JA
UK

Edward Elgar Publishing, Inc.
William Pratt House
9 Dewey Court
Northampton
Massachusetts 01060
USA

Paperback edition 2023

A catalogue record for this book
is available from the British Library

Library of Congress Control Number: 2022938914

This book is available electronically in the **Elgar**online
Sociology, Social Policy and Education subject collection
http://dx.doi.org/10.4337/9781803925615

MIX
Paper | Supporting
responsible forestry
FSC® C013604

ISBN 978 1 80392 560 8 (cased)
ISBN 978 1 80392 561 5 (eBook)
ISBN 978 1 0353 1695 3 (paperback)

Printed and bound by CPI Group (UK) Ltd, Croydon, CR0 4YY

Contents

Figures

Tables

Preface

The role of the public sector is central in all modern societies, including to solve a wide range of different tasks. Some tasks because they are not solved by others, and some because there is a desire that they are solved jointly and should not be left to the individual's ability to solve them.

At the same time, it is necessary to use resources as efficiently as possible. No country has unlimited opportunities to spend money on all the areas that everyone would like. There is therefore a need to prioritize – a task that will not become easier in the years to come.

This book should contribute to two things. One, to make it clearer that the public and private sectors are highly interdependent, and that each will not be able to be so effective without the other. The book therefore also argues that there may be social investments that are important for good societal development. The second is that the book can enable more people who find economics difficult to understand that it is crucial to know more about how best to prioritize resources, as well as to be aware of why we have a public sector and what tasks need to be solved.

My thanks go to the research group at RUC for their input, including especially to Camilla Jensen, Azhar Hussain and Nikolaj Christensen. Their advice has contributed a lot to the book's final structure and content. Any errors and omissions are, as usual, of course always the author's responsibility.

Bagsværd and Roskilde
January 2022
Bent Greve

1. The role of the public sector

1.1 INTRODUCTION

The aim of this book is to present public sector economics, including new ways of understanding the role of the public sector and the interaction between the public and private sectors. Further, it aims to show that the role of the state is in fact helpful to societal development by enacting what can be called social investment (such as childcare and long-term care and education). The public sector, due to the demand for private produced goods and services, is important for the private sector's jobs and production options. Support for research can also be part of the impact of public sector activities on the overall economic and societal development. Thus, this briefly shows that the public sector is not a burden for society, but when done in the right way, it is important for a solid economic societal development. Thereby also, the dynamic impact of public sector spending on societal development (in contrast to many other books in the field) has a stronger and more central role in the presentation, which covers not only the often argued possible negative impact on economic growth by the composition and level of taxes and duties, but also the need for a more balanced view of the role of the public sector. Still, good conditions for the private sector are important for societal development, for example, the creation of jobs, economic growth and the creation of income, that is, the public and private sector are highly dependent on each other.

This first chapter sets the stage for the book. It explains the book's approach on how to understand and analyse the public sector economy, while at the same time provides an overview of the book's chapters that may help the reader to understand the logic and context of the book. This includes as a central issue to constantly be aware that economics is about scarcity of resources, and the need to prioritize what should be produced, how to do it and by whom. Even in rich countries there is insufficient money available to fulfil all the wishes of citizens, interest groups and politicians wanting to be re-elected. As a consequence, money spent on one issue can't be spent on another issue and thereby a conflict will arise between different needs. Money is, at the end of the day, often the means necessary to achieve the ends, and naturally is not an aim in itself. This also implies that it is constantly important to think about how to most effectively use resources. If used more effectively, this will open the way for either lower taxes and duties and/or higher spending in other areas.

The economy of the public sector is further of central importance in all countries in order to make societies function in a wide range of, and very different, areas. Books about public sector economics often have a very high degree of detail and focus on the American economy in particular, see for example, Stiglitz and Rosengaard (2015), which is 923 pages long, or the now rather dated Holcombe (2006), Tresch (2008) or Musgrave and Musgrave (1973). In addition, they are often characterized by a significant degree of the application of mathematics and figures, which can make it difficult for some readers to get the necessary understanding of key economic and societal links between the public sector and society's overall economy. It can also be difficult to understand the opportunities for, as well as the consequences of, public sector intervention in society as a whole, including different types of arguments for why an intervention may have a positive or a negative impact on society's overall development. Further, public sector economics is often not a single subject for a book on economics, but is, instead, a narrow part of wider textbooks on economics where public sector economics plays only a limited role, as in Krugman and Wells (2018), despite this being a 985-page book.

The purpose of this book is thus to present concepts, possible causations and why economics of the public sector is central to understand the development of society, especially with a focus on European countries in a comprehensive, but still accessible, way. It does this without neglecting to ensure a solid insight into, and an understanding of, the theory of the role of the public sector, including management problems in relation to the public sector economy. It also links the issues and understanding of social investment to a stronger extent than often seen in books on the role of the public sector.

This chapter is structured so that in the next section just a few empirical data are presented. The purpose of this is to provide an insight into how much the public sector comprises the overall economy and core areas of spending. At the same time, it is important to be aware that size alone does not provide a clear description of the importance of the public sector economy for the overall economy. This is due to the fact, as repeated several times throughout the book, that public sector activity also involves the purchase of goods and services from private providers, and is often necessary for the private sector. Thus, the boundary as it is historically defined in national accounts may not even be a suitable border between the public and private sectors as both are dependent on each other. The public sector because public expenditure must be financed through taxes and duties, and the private sector, as mentioned, because the public sector buys goods and services, but also in a number of other areas, such as health, education, infrastructure and macroeconomic stability, to mention some of the most important. Here the public sector plays a vital role towards facilitating the proper or optimal functioning of the private sector. This is the focus in Section 1.2. Section 1.3 presents an overview of the book's chapters, and Section 1.4 points to a number of limitations. Section 1.5 concludes the chapter.

1.2   SIZE OF THE PUBLIC SECTOR – A FEW DATA

The fact that the government is important and influences societal development can be witnessed in Table 1.1, which shows revenue, net lending and expenditure and the highest and lowest levels in 2020.

A number of issues can be witnessed from this first overview of central information on the public sector. The first is that public sector spending is close to half of gross domestic product (GDP) in every year since 2011 in the EU-27 countries, but there is also strong variation in 2020. Secondly, that revenue has in none of the years been sufficient to finance the expenditure, albeit coming close in 2018 and 2019, and again with strong variations across countries. Thirdly, that different crises have had an impact on public sector economics. In 2011 and 2012 the higher level of spending and deficit are strongly related to the impact of the financial crisis, whereas in 2020 the impact of COVID-19 is the core reason for the strong increase in total spending and the increase in the level of deficit. Thus, the public sector is not only influenced by policy decision making, but also the impact of external shocks on the economies influences the position and options of the public sector.

Table 1.1 also indicates the wide variation of the size of the public sector, including that, over time, there will also be some relation between the spending and collection of revenue, so that in 2020 the highest spending was in France and the lowest in Ireland, whereas the highest revenue was in Denmark and the lowest in Ireland. There is, further, a very large difference in the size of the public sector. Deficits were lowest in Denmark and highest in Spain in 2020. Naturally, one needs to look into the data for individual years with caution, for example, especially in 2020 there was high impact on spending in all countries, but there might also in some years be extraordinarily high revenue for specific national reasons. One thus needs to look into national specificities to find out why there are changes and whether in a specific year there can be certain reasons for the development.

What to produce in the public sector, how to do it in the best way and in which more specific sectors of the economy are part of the analysis at several points in the book. However, as an indication of where the public sector on average spends money, Table 1.2 shows spending on the different areas, using the COFOG[1] system, as structuring the information on spending.

Table 1.2 shows that social protection, health and education are the overall largest areas of public sector spending, which is also a reason for looking at

Table 1.1 *Government revenue, borrowing and expenditure in EU-27 since 2011 and highest/lowest among the EU-27 countries in 2020*

TIME	2011	2012	2013	2014	2015	2016	2017	2018	2019	2020
Government revenue % of GDP	45.1	46.1	46.7	46.6	46.2	46.0	45.9	46.1	46.0	46.3
Highest 2020	**Denmark**	53.3								
Lowest 2020	**Ireland**	22.4								
Net lending (+) /net borrowing (−)	−4.1	−3.6	−2.9	−2.4	−1.9	−1.4	−0.8	−0.4	−0.5	−6.9
Highest 2020	**Denmark**	−0.2								
Lowest 2020	**Spain**	−11.0								
Government expenditure % of GDP	49.1	49.7	49.6	49.0	48.1	47.4	46.7	46.6	46.5	53.1
Highest 2020	**France**	61.6								
Lowest 2020	**Ireland**	27.4								

Source: Eurostat, GOV_10A_EXP, accessed 8 December 2021.

Table 1.2　　Public sector spending on different areas (COFOG) as % of GDP in EU28 countries (2010–19)

	Total	General public services	Defence	Public order and safety	Economic affairs	Environmental protection	Housing and community amenities	Health	Recreation, culture and religion	Education	Social protection
2010	50.1	6.8	1.5	1.9	5.2	0.9	0.9	7.3	1.2	5.2	19.3
2011	48.7	7.0	1.4	1.8	4.5	0.8	0.8	7.1	1.2	5.0	19.0
2012	49.1	7.0	1.4	1.8	4.7	0.8	0.7	7.1	1.1	5.0	19.3
2013	48.7	6.9	1.4	1.8	4.4	0.8	0.7	7.2	1.1	5.0	19.5
2014	48.0	6.7	1.3	1.7	4.3	0.8	0.6	7.2	1.1	4.9	19.3
2015	47.1	6.2	1.3	1.7	4.3	0.8	0.6	7.2	1.1	4.9	19.0
2016	46.4	6.0	1.3	1.7	4.1	0.8	0.6	7.1	1.1	4.8	19.0
2017	45.9	5.9	1.3	1.7	4.2	0.7	0.6	7.0	1.1	4.7	18.7
2018	45.7	5.8	1.3	1.7	4.3	0.8	0.6	7.1	1.1	4.7	18.6
2019	45.8	5.5	1.3	1.7	4.3	0.8	0.6	7.1	1.1	4.7	18.6

Source:　Eurostat, GOV_10A_EXP, accessed 8 December 2021.

areas in more detail later in the book. This is not the same in all countries and data can be blurred due to, just as one example, the fact that social benefits in some countries are taxable while in others they are not. This has an impact on both the level of spending and tax income in a country. These and related issues are discussed throughout the book.

1.3   OVERVIEW OF THE BOOK

A number of decisions on societies' development are influenced by ideological and political viewpoints. These include, as an example, the viewpoints related to minimum wage income, where liberals might see the value hereof, whereas neoconservatives might be more reluctant (Wilson 2021) and value the possible impact on labour supply higher. Here the focus mainly avoids more normative issues related to decisions, and instead tries to present how to analyse and answer questions about the best way to achieve the set goals. This is not to neglect the fact that there are normative perceptions about the role of the state, but this is mainly outside the scope of an economic analysis. The pros and cons of difficult options, including alternative costs, often better inform about economic consequences. This again does not neglect the fact that political positions and ideologies influence decisions.

After this first chapter, Chapter 2 focuses on allocation, distribution and stabilization as these are the three classic tasks for the public sector economy. The concepts are explained and described one by one, and then the chapter discusses where and how they might work in the opposite direction. This may mean, to exemplify, that a better distribution of a society's scarce resources can be achieved by an intervention in allocation, while at the same time there might be a risk of contributing to an increased degree of inequality. The difficulty of fulfilling a number of objectives at the same time thus becomes an illustration of the fact that a number of different types of intervention are often needed if several objectives of economic and societal development are to be achieved. Examples of intervention are presented, albeit specific instruments to achieve the goals are given later in the book.

Market failure, the focus of Chapter 3, is a key explanation for public intervention. The different types of market failures (imperfect competition, such as monopoly, natural monopoly, public goods, externalities and imperfect information, incomplete markets) are explained and exemplified. Unemployment and macroeconomic stabilization are also, at least by some, seen as market failures and are briefly depicted, while they are included in the presentation later in the book in relation to policy instruments in public sector economics. The chapter explains and gives examples of types of interventions that can help to reduce the consequences of these, including that interventions can and most often will have very different effects, which might even change over time. This given that market failures explain only a need for intervention, not what kind of intervention to choose, and, in theory, even so that it might be better to choose a more limited type of intervention. Further, market failures, for example, do not necessarily mean that there must be public production or changes in taxes and duties, but instead legal interventions such as prohibiting monopoly can be a way to cope with the issue. The choice of intervention must therefore be justified in itself and is not a consequence of the market not behaving like an invisible hand. Merit goods as a concept is also introduced, as well as examples of public services having the character of public goods. The risk of government failure is included as a contrast to market failure, but also, as returned to in Chapter 7, how the most effective way of using the scarce resources is achieved. Lastly, it discusses elements where there are disagreements about whether this is in fact market failure, such as inequality.

Section 1.2 has already presented a few data on the public sector, which are elaborated and discussed more in Chapter 4, by looking at issues such as: How large is the public sector in relation to other parts of the economy? This also includes how it is measured and defined in the national accounts. Does it matter, for example, whether the public sector itself produces or buys goods and services from private providers? Comparative European data also look at the difference in which areas have the most spent on them in different countries, that is, to illustrate that there does not have to be a specific use of resources and that there are, and will be, national differences in priorities. It also opens the way for a discussion as to how public expenditure can be perceived in some areas as investments in the future (e.g. research), or as elements that support labour supply, for example childcare, as this makes it possible for more people to be on the labour market. This is to illustrate that public activities can have different effects and are justified on the basis of various ways of understanding the interaction between the public and private sectors.

Public sector expenditures need to be financed and the overall demand in society regulated. Taxes, which are the focus of Chapter 5, play a central role in many and very different areas of a society. This applies, for example, in relation to labour supply, pollution and changes in the composition of consumption. In addition, there may be differences in the distributional effects of using different taxes and duties, while there must be a willingness to pay the necessary taxes and duties in order to finance the public sector. These possible conflicts and their impact on societies' development are discussed, including who, in fact, pays the different taxes and duties (the tax incidence). Lastly, taxation's possible impact on core issues such as labour supply and saving are included.

This leads naturally to a presentation of fiscal policy in Chapter 6, as this is a key instrument for the public sector to influence socio-economic development. The chapter looks at both automatic stabilizers and deliberate changes in public expenditure and revenue that can have a socio-economic impact. The multiplier effect is explained, including that the empirical analyses to understand the exact magnitude of the various effects are important, as the theory can only explain expected directions, but national variations and combinations of financing might have different impacts. Therefore, empirical analysis is extremely important in the analysis of public sector economics. Also discussed is which types of intervention can have the best effect based on what is the political desire to achieve, and which instruments can be the most effective ones to use given a specific goal of the intervention. The chapter also looks at how this can play together with the development of the business cycle and overall employment in a society. The impact of the international economy is integrated in Chapter 10.

Even when a decision has been made about what the public sector should deliver, there is a need for knowledge about how the public sector's economy can be managed in the best possible way so that maximum benefit comes from the public activities, which is the focus of Chapter 7. This requires knowledge of management methods, as well as how to get the best possible knowledge and make decisions based hereupon. Cost-benefit analysis is touched upon as an issue. Emphasis is placed on being able to explain possible reasons for inefficient production, as well as methods for obtaining the best possible knowledge as a background for decisions and possible ways to influence citizens' behaviour, for example, through and including in the presentation of behavioural economics. A possible instrument in this type of approach could be to use nudges. The principal–agent relationship is included in order to explain difficulties in managing and implementing public sector decisions, including conflicting perspectives between decision makers and policy groups.

In developed countries, social policy, health and education are the most expensive part of the public sector, as shown in Table 1.2. Chapters 8 and 9 look into the reasons for public sector involvement and what instruments to use within these areas. These three key areas of public sector activity are reviewed in some detail as they are of great importance for the overall development of society, and as mentioned often make up a very large part of the total public sector expenditure. In addition, these areas affect the individual's social and economic security. At the same time as being economic investments, for example, education and care of children have the character of social investments, which can contribute to society on a number of parameters, which are then enabled to function better than they would otherwise. Explanations of why the public sector finances these areas vary, but basically it is largely based on a merit good argument in conjunction with the fact that collective solutions can be socially cheaper than individual solutions. The chapters also discuss whether financing and producing the goods and services are connected. How to decide the overall level of spending and balance different needs and expectations are also part of the chapters. The split between the two chapters is based upon whether what they deliver is in-kind or in-cash. Chapter 8 focuses on the approaches to, and the understanding of, the impact, including different possible criteria for access to these benefits, whereas Chapter 9 looks into criteria, logics and the impact of delivering in-kind benefits, for example, different kinds of care.

The economy of the public sector is affected not only by the development of the nation state, but also by the international economic development, which is the focus of Chapter 10. The consequences for both financing and choice of expenses and possible investments in infrastructure are presented. The ways in which the Economic and Monetary Union influences are presented by a closer look at how this can influence the development of the public sector, and possible restrictions on national decision makers. Overall, European countries are covered as the ability to trade, take up loans and integration of labour markets influence societal development. Lastly, the requirements and possible size of the general government budget deficit and debt impact on the general government sector are discussed in the chapter.

Chapter 11 looks into the possible perspective of social investment. This is because looking into public economics also includes a focus not only on the short run, but also what might work in the longer-term perspective. This is part of the debate as to whether the public sector is a burden for societies or part of the solution for a better society. Thus, the chapter presents the idea of social investment, but also the possible difficulties in measuring this and the possible ethical challenges of using a social investment perspective in public sector economics. This also includes the issue of how investment in research and education can be part of how to ensure the good development of societies. Lastly, the chapter looks into the possible dynamic impact of public sector spending, including examples from a social investment perspective.

Finally, Chapter 12 discusses a number of the challenges facing the public sector in both the short and long term. A key challenge is the demographic development with an ageing population, which will be able to put pressure on, in particular, spending in relation to elderly care and healthcare. But also, how the public sector can be better prepared for international crises such as the financial crisis and the recent COVID-19 crisis is also included in the chapter. Lastly, the chapter discusses the legitimacy of the public sector and expected developments in the years to come.

1.4   A FEW DELIMITATIONS

For the sake of clarity, even if data are available on individual countries, as already also shown in this chapter, the book does not try to discuss national strategies, but will instead use national variations to indicate the possible variety in the way the public sector economics have an impact on societal development. This is further to indicate that there are options to choose from, and that public sector economics mainly deals with what from a theoretical perspective works, but also that institutions, history, ideology and traditions might imply variations in choice among countries.

This also includes that there are historical differences in the state's role as agents, including variations among countries between central and decentralized roles of the public sector, but this is not included. The political economy of the state is not included either, given the focus on an understanding of the role of the public sector and economic analysis with a focus on what can be done if one had an issue one would like to change. Still, one needs to be aware that there can be different roles for the states.

A discussion on whether we look into a Keynesian, neoclassical type of economic understanding as well as whether it is orthodox or heterodox is not central for the book, also because the sometimes-used argument that neoclassical theory is mainly pro-market is not correct. This further as these often more ideological differences are not central for understanding how and why there is public sector intervention as well as how they work. To further illustrate, it has been argued that one Nobel Prize winner, James Meade, "was a Keynesian in macroeconomics while embracing neo-classical microeconomics" (Hodgson 2019, 47). What is, however, included is the issue of whether incentives alone are related to money, including also discussions from behavioural economics.

Besides the regulations touched upon throughout the book, it might or could be argued that monetary policy can influence the economic development in societies. However, given the, by now in most countries, limited political influence on monetary policy, this is not included in the presentations, and, further, in Europe that central for the development, besides the influence of the global economic development, is the European Central Bank. Exchange rate policies are, for the same reasons, not part of the presentation in the book.

Theories of justice and the wanted size of redistribution will also at least implicitly imply a normative stance, and even though utilitarian understanding is presented, this is not central for the book, see instead Rawls (1972), Sen (1973) and Greve (2020). Still, when it comes to decisions in individual countries, ideological and political issues will have a role. The aim here is more to lay a foundation to understand the consequences as well as the arguments for the role of the public sector and its interaction with the rest of society.

There will always be uncertainty, and some might, in principle, be easier to estimate, whereas uncertainty related to, for example, events such as the financial crisis and COVID-19 is difficult to predict. There can therefore also be popular narratives influencing decision makers (Shiller 2017, 2021). Even though these elements exist and might have an impact on decisions, they will only to a very limited extent be included in the presentation.

1.5   CONCLUDING REMARKS

Central for this book is an understanding of the role of the public sector. The book uses a positive approach, that is, it describes the public sector economy, and then discusses the instruments available to cope with possible problems in society. The format is that if policy makers want to cope with an issue (whether allocation, stabilization or distribution) then the instruments that follow might be used, as well as the possible impact of using these instruments on a number of issues, such as equality, efficiency and public sector spending and deficits/debts.

It is further central to be aware that economics increasingly is an empirical matter, or as already stated a long time ago that "meaningful welfare economics of the welfare state must be empirical" (Sandmo 1995, 473). A consequence hereof is also that in individual countries, given the context and structure, one needs to analyse the impact of the consequence of interventions. However, it is still important to understand the concepts, theories and elements presented in the book, as this overall indicates the possible role of the public sector, without neglecting that policy makers might make decisions based on ideology more than theoretical and empirical knowledge. Still, it also implies a need to know how to interpret data, and therefore a number of data are used throughout the book in order to illuminate the role of the public sector for societal development.

NOTE

1.   COFOG is the Classification of the functions of government, see https://ec.europa.eu/eurostat/statistics-explained/index.php?title=Glossary:Classification_of_the_functions_of_government_(COFOG), accessed 8 December 2021.

REFERENCES

Greve, B. 2020. *Routledge International Handbook of Poverty*. Oxon: Routledge. https://doi.org/10.4324/9780429058103.
Hodgson, Geoffrey M. 2019. *Is There a Future for Heterodox Economics?: Institutions, Ideology and a Scientific Community*. Cheltenham, UK and Northampton, MA, USA: Edward Elgar Publishing.
Holcombe, Randall G. 2006. *Public Sector Economics: The Role of Government in the American Economy*. Upper Saddle River, NJ: Prentice Hall.
Krugman, Paul, and Robin Wells. 2018. *Economics*. New York: Macmillan Learning.
Musgrave, Richard Abel, and Peggy B. Musgrave. 1973. *Public Finance in Theory and Practice*. New York: McGraw-Hill.
Rawls, John. 1972. *A Theory of Justice*. Cambridge, MA: Harvard University Press.
Sandmo, A. 1995. "Welfare Economics of the Welfare State." *Scandinavian Journal of Economics* 97 (4): 469–76.

Sen, A. 1973. *On Economic Inequality*. Oxford: Clarendon Press.

Shiller, Robert J. 2017. "Narrative Economics." *American Economic Review* 107 (4): 967–1004.

Shiller, Robert J. 2021. "The Godley–Tobin Memorial Lecture." *Review of Keynesian Economics* 9 (1): 1–10.

Stiglitz, J., and J. Rosengaard. 2015. *Economics of the Public Sector*. 4th edn. London: W.W. Norton & Company.

Tresch, Richard W. 2008. *Public Sector Economics*. London: Macmillan International Higher Education.

Wilson, Shaun. 2021. *Living Wages and the Welfare State: The Anglo-American Social Model in Transition*. Bristol: Policy Press.

2. Allocation, distribution and stabilization

2.1 INTRODUCTION

This chapter focuses on allocation, distribution and stabilization, given these are the three classic tasks of the public sector according to the traditional view of the public sector's function (Musgrave and Musgrave 1989). The concepts are explained and described one by one, followed by a discussion as to where and how they can work in the same or opposite directions. This may mean, to exemplify, that a better distribution of a society's scarce resources can be achieved by an intervention in allocation, while at the same time there might be a risk that this will contribute to an increased degree of inequality. The difficulty of fulfilling a number of related objectives at the same time thus becomes an illustration of the fact that a number of separate types of interventions are often needed if several economic objectives, as well as other societal aims are to be achieved. Examples of intervention are presented, albeit specific instruments to achieve the goals are given later in the book. Still, as a continual issue that money spent on one activity can't be spent on another issue, that is, there are opportunity costs (which is also returned to throughout the book), the need to know how to prioritize spending is essential.

The chapter is organized, as indicated above, so that the focus in Section 2.2 is on allocation, in Section 2.3 on distribution and in Section 2.4 on stabilization, whereas Section 2.5 discusses the possible interaction between the three aims and the role of the public sector, and Section 2.6 concludes the chapter.

2.2 ALLOCATION

A central aim of public sector economics is to help in ensuring the best allocation of the scarce resources available. Society's resources have historically comprised three elements – labour, capital and land – and the use and interaction of all three in shifting proportions has implications on total production. The understanding of what can be produced is about the combination of labour and capital, which can be seen in the so-called Cobb-Douglas production function, first described in 1928 (Cobb and Douglas 1928), but also later used to explain the functional income distribution between wages and profit. This relation is not stable over the years, as it is, for example, influenced by technological developments. As an example, production in traditional industries needs less labour than previously due to the automation of production. This also shows that finding the best combination related to the preferences in a society and the most efficient allocation of scarce resources will not be a stable solution, as there will be a need for changes over time.

In recent years, the question of consumption/investment and its consequence, such as the impact on sustainable development for not only the economies, but also the environment, has been raised. Historically, however, pollution has been seen as an externality (see more in Chapter 3), but it does not change the fact that sustainability is increasingly included as an element as to where, how and in what way the public sector can affect the distribution of scarce resources. Thereby, the efficient use of resources is not only a short-term issue, but can also include longer-term perspectives on the consequence of using resources in different ways.

Another principle related hereto has been the Pareto criterion, which argues that allocation should be done as long as it can improve the situation for at least one person without reducing the options for any other persons. This can be seen as a very conservative criteria in the sense that following it strictly would imply that one should not take anything away from even the richest persons in order to change the allocation of resources. In modern times, the Pareto criterion is often used mainly as an indication that the state should at least influence the allocation when this makes it possible to improve the situation for at least one person without reducing it for other persons. Or if making the position worse for one person, it should compensate those in worse-off positions, the so-called Hicks criteria. Still, with the aim of totally increasing the utility in society.

The efficient allocation of resources, notwithstanding distributional issues, also implies that one should use production capacity in such a way that as much as possible is produced, given the production constraints. If there is a preference for more leisure, this might have an influence, although so far this has mainly influenced the labour supply of the individual and not the demand for goods and services in a society. This can be witnessed in Figure 2.1.

Figure 2.1 shows in a simple form the possible combination of the quantity of producing two goods (here butter and cheese) that can be produced with the use of available production factors. It also shows the production frontier, that is, the maximum production of different combinations of cheese and butter using the existing production resources. If a choice is made where the level of production is below the curve, such as point Y, then at least one person could be better off by moving the production to, for example, point X at the curve.

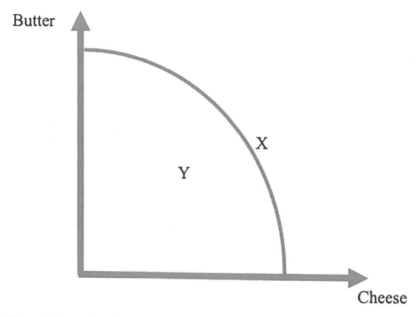

Figure 2.1   Production possibilities frontier when producing two goods

This is because at point X the production of goods is at least the same and higher for one of them than at point Y.

A further issue is the demarcation between the activities of the public and private sectors, which has been an issue since way back to Adam Smith (1776), including when and why the market would be able to deliver and use the scarce resources as best as possible. As Chapter 3 shows, Adam Smith was also aware that not all goods could be produced in the best way by the market.

Knowing that there is a need for influencing the allocation of resources does not inform us as to what way to do so. This is also because allocation is about both public and private production and investment as well as (returned to in Chapter 3) how to cope with a number of market failures and ensuring that competition is functioning in the private sector (in principle at least in some way also within the public sector). Thus, the difference between the possible available instruments and their more specific impact on the allocation of resources is the topic of a number of chapters later in the book.

As an illustration, changes in the allocation of resources can also be made in order to change consumption away from or towards certain goods and services.

2.3   THE DISTRIBUTIONAL ROLE

The public sector has the option to influence economic distribution in a society in many different ways. This does not imply that they will all be in agreement of interventions, or that the level of interventions will be to the same degree across the board. By using interventions in a number of different ways, the public sector can influence the degree of inequality, but also inequality over the life course, and thereby also functioning as a so-called piggy bank (Barr 2001). The decision on the degree of redistribution is usually normative, albeit there is and can be economic rational arguments for making redistribution as well, such as increasing demand and avoiding people living in poverty. Still, it implies that the degree of redistribution that is decided easily might be blurred by different ideological positions and opinions of the role of the state.

The distributional task is not only a question of monetary redistribution, but also of access to a number of services (e.g. care and nursing, health and education). The purpose of economic redistribution may also be to ensure that there is an opportunity to have money to buy the necessary consumer goods, although what the level of this should be is an open question. As people with high incomes have a higher savings ratio than people with low incomes, a redistribution from people with a high income to people with a lower income will also lead to an opportunity to increase the total consumption in an economy, and thus the total employment. The extent of this will, however, depend on the composition of consumption, that is, how much of it stems from domestic production and how much is imported.

Redistribution of resources in an economy can also affect society's overall level of utility. As illustrated in Figure 2.2, this is because it is generally assumed that there is a diminishing benefit of higher income (i.e. the marginal utility, MU in Figure 2.2) declining with the increase in disposable income, that is, income after the payment of income tax. This is due to the fact that once the basic needs have been met, additional goods and services will result in less growth in utility. For example, having another beer, ice cream, slice of bread, bicycle or a number of items after the first few will imply that they are less important and increases the marginal utility to a lesser extent than previous goods. The consequence of this is that if money is redistributed to people who have less disposable income, then the overall societal benefit (utility) will increase. Since we as individuals have different preferences, this does not mean that everyone should have the same amount. Furthermore, this is also due to the fact that there may be other consequences of redistribution, for example, related to incentives to work or save. These elements are seen a number of times throughout the book. So, even if we want to maximize society's utility at the outset, there may be other issues at stake to be aware of.

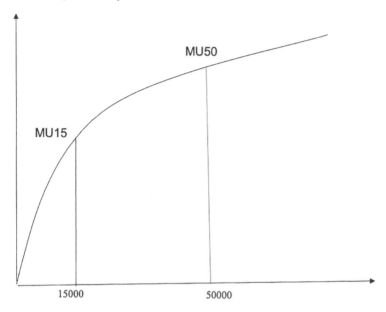

Total Utility of Consumption

MU50

MU15

15000   50000

Disposable income in EURO

Figure 2.2   Total utility and its relation to the disposable income

Figure 2.2 is naturally a stylized figure where the main aim is to illustrate that an increase in utility will diminish when getting higher levels of disposable income, and that higher total societal utility might be reached by a change in the degree of redistribution in a society. This has been argued to be central for a long time and even that maximizing utility would imply, as argued by Sidgwich already in 1874 (and here from another book) that "ultimately good was the 'greatest happiness of the greatest number'" (Kumekawa 2017, 20).

If there is a desire to influence the economic distribution, there may also be a need to know the extent to which there is economic inequality, including how inequality has developed over a number of years. This is also because it is not theoretically possible to argue that a certain level of inequality is correct, although it is known that a high degree of inequality can have negative effects on the way society functions, for example, in relation to crime and social coherence (see more in Aaberge and Brandolini 2015; Crouch 2019; Greve 2021).

There are many ways to measure economic inequality. The approach that is the most used in the literature (Greve 2021) and with easy access to data (such as from Eurostat and Organisation for Economic Co-operation and Development (OECD)) is the Gini coefficient. In recent years, there has also been a greater focus on how much the richest earn and how much wealth they have. Therefore, for example, there is also data for how large a share of both income and wealth the richest 1 per cent has, see for example https://wid .world/. Other measures include the income of the 20 per cent with the highest income compared to the 20 per cent with the lowest – called the 80/20 ratio. They often, as well as other measures, give the same results as a consequence of the same data being used for the calculations. If using measurements having a stronger normative perspective of which group to support with redistribution, this can have an impact.

Regardless of which measurement method is used, there are and will always be a number of measurement problems, including whether there should be a focus on individuals or families, how hidden activities in the economy are included, whether data for one year is sufficient to assess the degree of inequality. But at the same time, using the same method over a number of years tells something about how the development changes. Therefore, it is a valuable calculation to make, as it provides information about whether a society is moving in a more equal or unequal direction.

One specific problem is that the value of public service is not typically included when measuring the degree of inequality, because (among other things), for example, the cost of having a hospital treatment can, despite being of high value, not be converted and used for buying goods and services. Also not included in the information on the degree of inequality are private expenditures in order, for example, to pay for healthcare, including payment for private insurances, if there are no or limited services provided by the public sector. This is because those with higher risk (see more in Chapter 9) of unemployment or having bad health will have to pay more for insurance.

The Gini coefficient has a value between 0 and 1. If the value is 0, the distribution is completely equal and if it is 1, the distribution is completely unequal. The numbers are often seen as being between 0 and 100 (Gini index), but it is still true that the larger the number, the higher the inequality.

It can also be illustrated graphically, as in Figure 2.3, as a Lorenz curve. In Figure 2.3 the straight line (the 45-degree curve) shows a complete equal distribution. Inequality is measured by, in principle, putting all citizens on a line starting with the lowest income up to the highest income. To the extent that someone has a smaller share, they will also have a smaller share than their share of the population. Thus, the first 10 per cent of the population has approximately 3 per cent of the income in the figure, and the richest 10 per cent around 25 per cent of the income. The area between the 45-degree line and the curved curve as proportion of the total area below the 45-degree line is the Gini coefficient and thus the further down the figure it slopes, the greater the degree

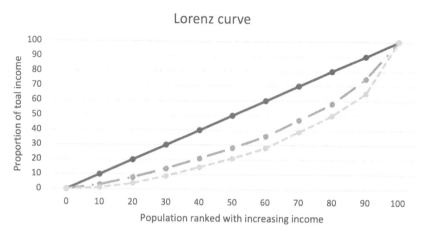

Figure 2.3   The Lorenz curve – a stylized example

of inequality in the distribution. The two sloped lines in the figure indicate that there is a higher level of inequality in the distribution where the curve is constantly below the other curve. If the curves intersect, one will have to analyse and indicate the preference as to where in the distribution one prefers to have the highest level of inequality.

Overall, public sector activities in most developed nations redistribute resources both between rich and poor (the Robin Hood effect), but also across generations, so that the redistribution often takes place to children and the elderly, with those of working age paying more. The distribution is more unequal if it is related to wealth (Kuypers, Figari, and Verbist 2021).

2.4   STABILIZATION

By the use of interventions, the state can help in ensuring a more stable economic development, even if it is the case that not all agree that this is the task of the public sector. This has now been a debate for a long time, and the risk of not ensuring a stable economic development was pointed out after both the First and Second World Wars by John Maynard Keynes (Carter 2021). Keynes is also often seen as the one arguing for an active fiscal policy intervention to modify business cycles.

Stabilization is about not only balancing cyclical fluctuations, but also basically trying to contribute to a number of economic balances, including the current account of the balance of payments, as well as employment and unemployment. In addition, for most economies in Europe, there is a consideration to take into account public budget deficits and debt (see more in Chapter 10).

In addition, inflation developments may be taken into account, although until 2021 this has not been a key consideration, as prices have risen very slowly and at the same time there have been negative interest rates in a number of countries. Rising inflation influences distribution and there is a risk for some of living in poverty as their income is not necessarily increased to the same extent as inflation.

In the short term, stabilization policies can consist of fiscal, monetary and exchange rate policies, although the possible mix in each country depends on preferences and the degrees of national freedom. For example, for members of the European Monetary Union there is no possibility to use exchange rate policies, and also, at least for smaller countries, monetary policy is available only to a more limited degree.

In the rest of the book, public sector economy stabilization focuses in particular on the more short-term opportunities where finance policy could have an impact. In principle, growth and structural policy may also have long-term opportunities to influence stabilization. However, certain elements of a more long-term nature, such as spending on infrastructure, research and education, are partly discussed later in the book including in relation to the social investment perspective.

2.5   DO THEY INTERACT?

As a general rule, an instrument can only solve one problem, while at the same time there may be a risk that it will create another problem. This means that if a number of socio-economic problems are to be solved, it may be necessary to use a number of instruments to solve both identified problems and the possible new problems created by an intervention.

Theoretically, we know, for example, that incentives to take a job can be affected by the level of income transfers, so that the distance in disposable income between having a job and being on an income benefit can affect the labour supply. On the other hand, the question about how large a distance there should be is an empirical one, for example, because working is not only a matter of income, but also of having something to get up for in the morning and the opportunity often for a social community with others. Economic theory thus does not stand alone as a possible explanation of behaviour, even though preferences for leisure and relations to other persons can be included, albeit this can be difficult to monetize. At the same time, behaviour is affected by the fact that individuals have different preferences. For some, there must be a big difference for it to affect behaviour and, for others, just a small difference.

An increase in income transfers to unemployed can, for example, contribute to the stabilization of economies, as was seen in a number of countries during the COVID-19 crisis to keep consumption up (and thus also employment).

Unemployment benefits can also work as an automatic stabilizer (see more in Chapter 6). This while higher levels of benefits may, for some, have meant that they worked or searched for jobs to a lesser extent than they otherwise would have done. The possible incentives of changes in benefits as well as different kind of taxes and duties are returned to throughout the book.

There will, therefore, almost always be both intended and unintended effects of a number of economic interventions with the aim of influencing either allocation, distribution or stabilization. Economic theory can describe the expected direction, but the empirical analyses can help to qualify the magnitude in different contexts. Thus, one will have to analyse different types of interventions in order to qualify and discuss whether and how they will influence allocation, distribution and stabilization.

2.6 CONCLUSION

Allocation, distribution and stabilization are key objectives for the public sector's various forms of economic intervention in society as a whole and in the way the market operates.

Central to this is that there are a significant number of instruments available if it is desired to influence the development of society, but at the same time it is given that intervention in one part of society to achieve a goal can have an impact in other areas. Therefore, interventions require careful consideration of not only the desired effects, but also the possible risk of unwanted effects. Variations in the instruments used to achieve the goals will run through a number of chapters in the book, including the possible advantages and disadvantages hereof.

REFERENCES

Aaberge, Rolf, and Andrea Brandolini. 2015. "Multidimensional Poverty and Inequality." In *Handbook of Income Distribution*, edited by A.B. Atkinson and F. Bourguignon, Vol. 2A: 141–216. Amsterdam: Elsevier.

Barr, N. 2001. *The Welfare State as a Piggy Bank. Information, Risk, Uncertainty, and the Role of the State.* Oxford: Oxford University Press.

Carter, Zachary D. 2021. *The Price of Peace: Money, Democracy, and the Life of John Maynard Keynes.* New York: Random House Trade Paperbacks.

Cobb, Charles W., and Paul H. Douglas. 1928. "A Theory of Production." *The American Economic Review* 18 (1): 139–65.

Crouch, Colin. 2019. "Inequality in Post-Industrial Societies." *Structural Change and Economic Dynamics* 51: 11–23.

Greve, B. 2021. *Multidimensional Inequalities. International Perspectives across Welfare States.* Berlin: De Gruyter.

Kumekawa, Ian. 2017. *The First Serious Optimist. A.C. Pigou and the Birth of Welfare Economics.* Princeton, NJ: Princeton University Press.

Kuypers, Sarah, Francesco Figari, and Gerlinde Verbist. 2021. "Redistribution in a Joint Income–Wealth Perspective: A Cross-Country Comparison." *Socio-Economic Review* 19 (3): 929–52.

Musgrave, R., and P. Musgrave. 1989. *Public Finance in Theory and Practice*. New York: McGraw-Hill.

Smith, Adam. 1776. *An Inquiry into the Wealth of Nations*. *Book*. 1970 edn. London: J.M. Dent & Sons Ltd, Everymans Library. https://doi.org/10.7208/chicago/9780226763750.001.0001.

3. Market failure and other reasons for public interventions

3.1 INTRODUCTION

Market failure is a key explanation for public sector intervention in the economy. There are a number of different types of market failures (imperfect competition, such as monopoly), natural monopoly, public goods, externalities and imperfect information, incomplete markets), which are all explained and exemplified in this chapter, albeit the chapter starts with a very short presentation of the key conditions needed for the market to work. Not all interventions are for purely economic reasons, but they might also be due to a wish to reduce the possible political power of very large companies, such as those arising from new technology, including the collection of information (Susskind 2020).

Unemployment and macroeconomic development are also seen, at least by some, as market failures and are depicted, albeit very briefly, because they are included in the presentation later in the book in relation to different policy instruments available for nation states. Still, the chapter explains and gives examples of types of interventions that can help to reduce the consequences of these, including that various types of interventions can and most often will have very different effects, as also argued in Chapter 2 with regard to allocation, distribution and stabilization. The reason for including this is that market failures show only the need for intervention, not what kind of intervention to choose and, in theory, even that it might sometimes be better to choose a more limited type of intervention.

Further, market failures do not necessarily mean that there must be public production or changes in taxes and duties, but instead legal interventions such as legally prohibiting monopolies and doing what is possible to reduce the risk hereof. The choice of intervention must therefore be justified in itself and is not a consequence of the market not behaving like an invisible hand.

Merit goods as a concept is also introduced, as well as examples of public services having the character of public goods. The risk of government failure is also included as a contrast to market failure, but also (as returned to in Chapter 7) that the most effective way of using scarce resources needs to be central both when using the market and the public sector to produce goods and services. Lastly, the chapter discusses elements where there are disagreements about whether this is in fact market failure, such as unemployment, macroeconomic stabilization and inequality.

One argument for imposing public changes to activities is that they should be made as long as they can improve the position of at least one person without compromising the situation of others (the Pareto criterion). As argued in Chapter 2, this can't theoretically be the only criterion to use given also the possible conflict with distributional issues.

The chapter proceeds by presenting in Section 3.2 conditions for a competitive market, and then in Section 3.3 looking into the classical market failures. Section 3.4 looks into merit goods, Section 3.5 looks into issues related to unemployment and inequality, before Section 3.6 discusses government failures. Lastly, Section 3.7 concludes the chapter.

3.2   CONDITIONS FOR A WELL-FUNCTIONING MARKET

In classical economics textbooks there are a number of conditions that should be fulfilled in order to have a well-functioning market. Simply said, a well-functioning market requires that there are many buyers and sellers who basically act rationally. There is full transparency and there is no one who alone or together with a few others can influence the price of the goods.

Individuals want to maximize their utility and companies want to maximize profits. Given (as described in Chapter 2) that there is declining marginal utility with higher income, as well as budget restrictions in the individual household, the demand for goods will fall with rising real prices because there is no available income for the individual to buy the same amount of goods as before if consumption of other goods continues at the same level. Also, as when prices are higher the marginal utility of an extra unit will decline, given there might be others then giving more utility for the level of income. Correspondingly, producers of goods will increase production as long as the price in the market is higher than the marginal cost of producing this unit. Therefore, with higher prices they will produce more and with lower prices they will produce less. Thus, when both supply and demand are elastic, that is, that the quantity bought and sold changes with the change in prices, then the changes in demand and supply with these changing prices will end up in an equilibrium both for quantity and price, which at the same time contributes to societal efficiency (see Chapter 2). Although it is a very strong condition related to rational behaviour, which is rarely fully met in practice, it is nevertheless the case that both consumers and producers will typically react to how the situation on the market is. If the price of an item goes up, then people will buy less and, overall, there will be less demand in the market. Manufacturers also prefer to produce if they can get such a good price for a product that they can make a profit, and therefore typically produce and sell more with higher prices. This is also the explanation as to why changes in taxes, for example, have an impact on the way the market works (discussed in more detail later in the book). The traditional demand and supply curve in a well-functioning market is shown in Figure 3.1.

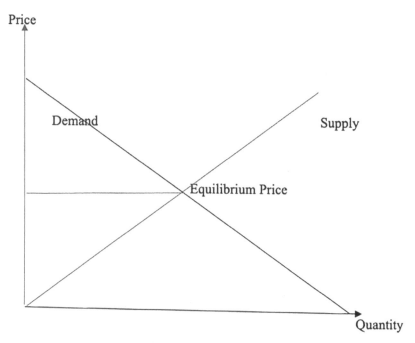

Figure 3.1   Equilibrium in a market for goods

The equilibrium price and quantity in Figure 3.1 is where the price equals the marginal costs, as it is assumed that there are growing marginal costs as well as declining marginal utility for consumers.

It is the case that the market works best in areas where buying goods and services is frequent, and the price and quality of the goods are known by consumers. It also explains why, for example, that also even if there is free choice of welfare state services this may not work for everyone in all areas (Greve 2010; Dursin et al. 2021). Most will depend on advice and guidance, for example in relation to healthcare. If there is a large transaction cost and/ or that producers have incentives to cream-skim, that is, take the easiest cases with the highest profit and leave the more difficult cases to other providers, then it might be working less well. This is also why, for a long time, there have been discussions on how quasi-markets, that is, not fully competitive markets, actually function (Bartlett and Le Grand 1993).

A perfectly functioning market also requires that there is perfect information available, making it possible for the individual to take informed decisions. Information also needs to be available in such a way that individuals can easily get access to it.

Thus, even if the perfect conditions are not fulfilled, the market will function in many parts of everyday life and will react, for example, on signals from changes in prices on the selling and buying of goods and services. This also is a reason why, even if not all buyers or sellers constantly act rationally, the market can still function relatively well. Especially in cases where goods and services are bought frequently, and less so for more complicated issues and for elements individuals buy only very seldomly or perhaps only once in a lifetime, there is higher risk that buying goods is influenced by non-rational behaviour, but also including the fact that having perfect information might be more difficult. In certain markets it is even the case that the buyer will be dependent on the advice of the sellers – for example, car repairs or medical treatment – and this might imply supplier-induced demand.

Overall, even if the market provides valuable information, in a number of cases markets do not function properly, which is the focus in the next section.

3.3   MARKET FAILURES

Markets fail for a number of reasons. Market failure is still, and has been for a long time, a core argument for public sector intervention, even though not necessarily which type of corrections to use (Smith 1776; Keynes 1936; Forte and Peacock 1985; Stiglitz and Rosengaard 2015). It is then central to get an idea about what market failures are and the different types hereof.

Stiglitz and Rosengaard (2015) list six items that they label basic market failures:

1. Imperfect Competition
2. Public Goods
3. Externalities
4. Incomplete Markets
5. Imperfect Information
6. Unemployment and other Macroeconomic Disturbances (Stiglitz and Rosengaard 2015, 93)

Given the disagreement among economists of whether the last issue is a market failure, it is not included in the presentation below, but is still discussed later in the chapter (see Section 3.5). Some would also argue that merit goods is a market failure, but again due to disagreements hereabout, this is discussed in a separate section (Section 3.4). The individual subsections below discuss the other five basic market failures.

There are various possible explanations why market failure can occur. This may be because it is not possible to charge for the goods, which applies to public goods, as there will be no possibility of maintaining property rights, and thus that some can enjoy the goods without paying for them (free-rider). Free-ride can be reduced for private goods as there can be property rights, but in reality is not possible for public goods. There are also areas with economies of scale or increasing returns to scale (natural monopolies), where it would be a waste of societal resources to have more producers. There may be costs that are not included in the price (see more in the section on externalities). Lastly, there is, for example, the infrastructure which, once established (as long as there is no queue on the road/bridge, etc.) will be the best route to use, for the sake of the economy, and thus in order for this to happen the price theoretically must be zero because there are no extra costs (the marginal cost of one extra user is zero). Thus, for example, an extra car using a bridge implying that more people take advantage of it should not imply a fee. This can therefore also be a rationale for the public sector that builds the bridge to ensure that as many people as possible use it, at least until there is congestion. Naturally, if there is a running cost of keeping the bridge maintained then this can be charged to the users by means of a fee for using the bridge, which is equal to the marginal running cost.

It is important to emphasize that because there are market failures this does not in itself inform what type of public sector regulation should be made. The different forms and opportunities for public intervention vary from the public sector producing the goods itself to making demands on how they are produced, as well as the possibility of influencing prices of specific products through various taxes and duties. The type of instruments that can be used are included in a number of chapters later in the book. In addition, even if the public sector produces the goods, there will be a need to find out how much is to be produced and under what conditions they are to be used, for example in the form of user fees or restrictions in who gets access to the goods. The size of production is looked at in more detail throughout the book, including in Section 3.6.

3.3.1   Imperfect Competition

Imperfect competition refers to the existence of monopoly or monopoly-like conditions, with the consequence that prices become higher because one who can set the price in a market as a monopolist can and will take a higher price because they are the only provider or because other providers cannot offer the consumer the commodity at lower price. The price thus becomes higher than what consumers are willing or able to pay, and the prices are set higher so that more money can be earned for the company than under perfect competition.

It does not have to be just one company, but it can be several companies that have a common interest in a higher price, or whose products differ slightly from each other, that is, monopolistic competition, including that the difference implies a possible degree of substitution to the other product, while still they are each close to having a product that no one else can deliver.

In addition, there are what can be described as natural monopolies. These are situations where it is cheaper for one company to produce all products (i.e. single supplier) because there is high fixed cost, economies of scale in production, no substitutes (and thus demand being price inelastic) and high barriers to entry. This also implies that the marginal cost of producing an extra unit goes towards zero when production increases. In addition, it would be too expensive for societies, for example, to increase the number of sewers, water pipes and other supply units. Therefore, states are often the ones investing in infrastructure, including water, electricity, roads, bridges and heating. Thus, there will also be a need to decide what the payment should be for these products. Prices might reflect the fact that there shall be no profit from this production, and if there is a profit and it is state-owned it can, in principle, be compared to a tax on this product. Further, that even though it makes sense that, for example, railway tracks are only laid in one place, it is not a given that it must be the same companies that run trains on the rail tracks, indicating that a combination of natural monopolies with competition can be a possibility.

Naturally, due to technological development a good might not continue to be a natural monopoly, such as what has historically been the case with lighthouses and television signal distribution.

A growing issue is that due, especially, to new technology, there has been a rise in the market power in a number of areas with very large international firms (Eeckhout 2020), implying a stronger need in order to avoid the possible negative repercussions on societies' development from monopolies through state interventions – and even global agreements might be necessary to ensure international competition. This topic is returned to several times throughout the book.

3.3.2   Public Goods

There are products where it is difficult, or even impossible, to charge a price for such a good, often labelled public goods. A public good is characterized by the fact that one person's consumption of the good does not prevent others from using that good (non-rivalry). Consequently, one can also not prevent people from using the good in question, and therefore it would not be possible

Table 3.1   *Goods dependent on exclusion and rivalry is possible or not*

Consumption goods characteristics	Exclusion	
	Feasible	Not feasible
Rival	1 Private goods (e.g. food, clothes)	2 "Club-goods" (e.g. roads, bridges with user fees)
Non-rival	3 Common (e.g. libraries, some sports facilities)	4 Public goods (e.g. defence, police, judiciary)

Source: Elaborated from Musgrave and Musgrave (1989).

for a private provider to charge a price for the good. This applies to classical issues such as air and water, but also the production of, for example, the judiciary and military. The fire service is another example, where the risk is if only those who have paid for insurance are helped in case of a fire, the fire may become more extensive as some houses will continue to burn which can then spread again.

This was already recognized by Adam Smith, that there would be goods and services where a private producer would not be able to get a profit or even to cover the cost of production, and, thus there would need to be a public provision of these goods (Smith 1776).

The classic areas are the diplomatic service, police, defence and justice, which are often called pure public goods.

Table 3.1 exemplifies the distinction between private and public types of markets depending on whether or not it is possible to exclude persons from using the good, and whether the consumption by one person reduces the options of other persons using the good (rivalry).

Table 3.1 also illustrates that there may be fluid boundaries and also that there may be goods and services whose character changes over time. The fluid boundaries are exemplified in cases 2 and 3 where, in case 2, consumption is rival and where, except when imposing user charges, exclusion is not feasible. In case 3, up to a certain limit one person's use does not reduce another person's use hereof, albeit there might be times where there are no library books available or free time at a sports facility, and also thus if private exclusion from use is possible, including charging fees might be possible, such as in sports centres.

A good can, as mentioned, change place in the scheme over time. A classic example is lighthouses. Initially, no payment could be charged for this, as everyone could see the lights and use them. With modern technology to help in manoeuvring ships, payment can be charged for the service, and thus the good has moved from a pure public good to a private good. The same is the case for the development in television.

Other changes in boundaries relate to the fact that, for example (as mentioned above), we perceive clean air as a public good, but at the same time pollution of the air is a negative externality (Nelson 1985). There are also goods which it is possible at first to use without difficulties (new roads, bridges, for example) but which, over time, are used by more people, which then reduces this option. This has been labelled positional goods (Hirsch 2013).

There can also be regional variations in access to public goods, such as cultural facilities that are only available in one part of a country.

As returned to in later chapters, a public good (such as police and military) does not imply that the good as a whole is produced publicly. The military and police thus buy a number of the elements they use through the market, such as food, clothes and other equipment. Thus, public goods are a reason for state intervention because if left to the market they would either not be produced or be at risk of not being taken care of (air and water, for example), but they do not inform about how to make the intervention. The decision on what to produce and under what conditions needs then to be made, albeit that pure public goods are normally produced within the public sector.

3.3.3   Externalities

A distinction can be made between positive and negative externalities. The most used in analysis are the negative ones. They consist of the fact that when companies produce and have to sell their goods and services, they only include the direct costs of the company when producing the good. However, if the company pollutants emit a high level of CO_2, then the environmental cost is not automatically included in the company's costs, and thus the price of the product. The classic example is companies that discharge wastewater into a river, causing the river to become polluted so that anglers can no longer catch fish. The negative consequences for anglers are not automatically included in the price of the company's products. So, fundamentally, negative externalities are about the fact that there are societal costs that are not included in companies' prices unless society regulates those costs in one way or another. This can be, for example, through taxes and duties, but also legal regulation on, for example, the size of acceptable emissions or content of toxic substances in certain goods, such as phthalates used in producing some toys.

Conversely, there are also positive externalities. This is the case, for example, with vaccines, which were most recently recognized during the COVID-19 crisis, because the more people who have been vaccinated, the less the risk of spreading diseases. Similarly, there can be positive effects for others of joint activities, such as when more people have an education, society often works better.

Thus, there are strong reasons to try to cope with externalities, albeit which instrument to use depends on a more precise analysis of the specific case where one needs to balance the cost of intervention with the goal of reducing negative externalities or supporting positive ones. Thus, for example, removing all types of pollution might be too costly compared to the societal gain by reducing it. Only an empirical analysis can inform about how strong the intervention should be. Still, it is the case, as argued already by Pigou a long time ago, that these divergences related also to the difference in marginal utility and marginal cost to change this, because: "It is, however, possible for the State if it so chooses, to remove the divergence in any field by 'extraordinary encouragements' or 'extraordinary restraints' upon investment in that field. The most obvious forms which these encouragements and restraints may assume are, of course, those of bounties and taxes" (Pigou 1950, 192). Therefore, later in the book, different instruments – especially tax instruments – that can have an impact are returned to.

Externalities might not only relate to national borders. Environmental issues are often transnational as pollution in one country can have an impact in another country. So can the use of fiscal policy. This is because "fiscal policy can have spillovers in the sense that a fiscal expansion or contraction in one country might affect not only domestic output but also output in the other country" (Blanchard, Leandro, and Zettelmeyer 2021, 13). This might also have implications for which policy is enacted as well as the need for international cooperation in economic policy (see also Chapter 10).

3.3.4 Incomplete Markets

This can be a market where, for example, the demand for goods is so low that producers do not find it profitable to produce them because this requires a high price where few persons would be willing or able to pay for the product. This might be in remote areas where few people are living, very specific products for persons with disabilities or certain types of sickness.

It can also be the case that certain risks can not be covered by insurance, and whether they will come with a very high price. This is due to adverse selection, which originally referred to when buying lemons one does not know whether one gets a bad lemon among the good lemons. Therefore, problems with selling insurance may be because the person who is to sell the insurance does not know whether the buyer of the insurance has a higher risk of, for example, becoming ill or unemployed. This is labelled adverse selection.

Related to this is also whether persons who have taken out insurance behave less sensibly (e.g. riskier in terms of health or in relation to keeping their job). This is called moral hazard.

In addition, from a distributional point of view, using the private insurance market will mean that people with higher unemployment rates than others will have a high risk of having to pay a higher price than people with a lower risk of becoming unemployed. This is further because if it is known which groups have a lower risk than others, they will try to band together to take out an insurance where, due to their smaller risk, they can become insured for a smaller premium than others with a higher risk of unemployment.

Overall, this points to the need for public intervention without it being clear exactly what type of intervention it should be.

3.3.5   Imperfect Information

These are to a large extent elements that, directly or indirectly, are also included in a number of other elements of market failure. Basically, if there is not enough and clear information then the buyers cannot make the best choice. Information can consciously or unconsciously not be perfect, or even be misleading about, for example, the quality or content of a product.

These are areas that are typically regulated in many countries through legislation and requirements for information about what a product contains, for example, additives, or whether the product can have harmful consequences for allergy sufferers or the environment.

Good and accurate information that is easy to access can also be perceived as a form of public good, as several people can use the same information without preventing others from using it.

Imperfect information might also include that the quality of a good or service is only more limited to be informed about, making choices more difficult.

3.4   MERIT GOODS

Merit goods can be defined as goods that, if production is left solely to the market, will be produced in a lower quantity than what society would prefer in order to have the best welfare development. The first example, proposed by Richard Musgrave in 1959, to be used (and still is in many countries) is the example of luncheon vouchers to children in schools to ensure that they get sufficient nutrition. This is still today considered important in several countries as a way to ensure that children not only get healthy food, but also are able to follow teaching. Sometimes, this also implies that taxpayers might be more willing to finance in-kind services, as they then know what the money is used for, which is not the case for direct income transfers. This is a paternalistic view on what individuals are willing to pay for and can also be a societal view on the fact that there is need for state intervention to ensure a sufficient high level of provision of certain goods, such as education (see Chapter 9).

The provision of education today is one such example of merit goods, as in principle there could be a market for the provision of education with many buyers and suppliers, but also implying a risk that many will not be able or willing to pay for an education, especially further education, and, thus the overall level of human capital would be lower than what is optimal in society in order to ensure future employability and level of production.

Still, the issue and question is how the optimal solution is then found, which is an issue to be returned to in Section 3.6 on government failures, and in later chapters. In many ways, this is a classical issue in public sector economics that one knows that interventions can be important for societal development, however the size hereof can be more difficult to depict, as well as what quality the service should have. This implies that decisions are often not only economic issues, but also dependent on preferences from decision makers. Still, economics can inform on why intervention is important, as well as the fact that empirical studies can help in prioritizing between different kinds of interventions. See also more in Chapter 11 with regard to the issue of social investment.

3.5   UNEMPLOYMENT, INEQUALITY AND OTHER SOCIETAL IMBALANCES

In a number of areas, there is overwhelming agreement that societal interventions are needed to ensure a well-functioning society. It is about unemployment, inflation and other societal imbalances (e.g. the balance of payments), but it can also be seen in relation to the environment, which, however, as a result of negative externalities in production is already a reason for societal intervention. There is also a discussion on whether the public sector should intervene in order to change the level of inequality.

Most agree that it would be good to avoid a high level of unemployment, including because production resources, such as labour, that are not used result in a societal loss of production that cannot be recovered later. There is also (see more in Chapters 8 and 9) a negative influence on the quality of life by being unemployed, which can reduce the level of happiness in a country, including for some social exclusion from society. There is albeit not necessarily agreement on the degree and need for public sector intervention.

This is because, in simplified form, there are two explanations for the risk of unemployment. One often described as liberal, finds as a starting point that unemployment is due to the fact that there are wage earners who demand too high a wage, and that if they were willing to work for the current wage within their area, then they would be able to get jobs, or that their productivity is below the minimum income, implying that they will not get a job. In such an understanding, the argument is that unemployment will automatically decline when an adjustment takes place in relation to wage expectations.

In the second understanding, often referred to as Keynesian, a central explanation for unemployment is that there is a lack of demand in the economy. In such a situation, during periods of high unemployment, the public sector can influence overall unemployment through changes in public spending or in the tax system.

Similarly, if the economic development means that there is a risk of such a very high level of economic activity that there will be a shortage of labour, the public sector will be able to dampen demand through higher taxes and fees or lower public expenditure, which is looked at in more detail in Chapter 5.

Overall, there is no doubt that the public sector has the potential to influence the overall employment development of a country. Similarly, the public sector can influence the degree of economic inequality in a country, which is seen in relation to taxes and duties in Chapter 5, and for public activities especially in relation to services in Chapter 8, and income transfers in Chapter 4. However, a priori, we do not know what the "optimal" degree of economic inequality is, but we do know that there can be negative impact on societies' developments (see also Greve 2021).

Other issues include the current account of the balance of payments. Here, fiscal policy by reducing activities, for example, can also imply an option to reduce imports of goods and services and thereby improve the balance. Overall sustainability for societal development can also be influenced by the public sector, as already touched upon with regard to negative externalities.

3.6   GOVERNMENT FAILURES

Just as there are market failures, there is also a risk that there are government failures. Central here is that there is no unambiguous way of calculating how great the demand for the public sector goods and services is, including whether and how re-election in the political system can affect decision makers' preferences for where and to whom more income transfers and services are to be directed. This, especially from Public Choice theorists, has led to the argument that the public sector is like the sea monster, Leviathan (Hobbes 1980; Mueller 1987).

In addition, there are arguments that the bureaucracy has its own interests in more money coming into its area (Niskanen 1971), which in many countries is limited by the fact that there is a Ministry of Finance whose task is to try to manage the overall expenditure development within the framework that there is a willingness among the citizens to finance. The risk of larger expenses than what is desirable overall may also be that interest groups, and often with good results for their groups, push for more expenses.

This contributes to what is called asymmetric growth in public spending if one can argue for large gains for a particular group while keeping the total increase in public spending for all limited, or with an amount that compared to the overall level of public sector spending seems like a tiny amount. For example, if larger expenses for a small group of citizens, which give them much better conditions, alone may cost 2 Euro per month per capita, this may be easier to get acceptance for. The public sector difficulty is that there can be many of these types of activities and if they are all decided upon it can be many Euro per capita. At the same time, in these as in other areas, the simple statement applies that money spent in one area cannot be used in another area.

In addition, as in the private sector, there is a risk of the inefficient use of resources, which means that there will also be a need in the public sector for analysis of, and control over, the most optimal use of resources. Inefficiencies can occur in many and different ways, but for example there may be new technology which means that the work can be performed in a different and better way than before.

As a consequence, it is not possible to say anything in advance about the extent of public failures, only that they may be there, and this is due both to the fact that preferences are not known and can be difficult to depict. Asking people about their willingness to pay is difficult, and the answer can be different if it is actually a good one prefers or does not prefer, so this makes the revelation of preferences difficult. Higher spending might also be a consequence of pressure groups and bureaucracy, and that there is therefore a need to constantly weigh resource consumption within the individual areas of the public sector. Furthermore, people might say they are in favour of increased spending if they are asked, without, at the same time, asking whether they are willing to pay more in taxes and duties (OECD 2021).

3.7   CONCLUDING REMARKS

The chapter has looked at a number of explanations for why there is a public sector in all countries and why it is necessary to take into account the best use of scarce resources in order to make interventions in the way the market works. Central to this are market failures, but also important are issues related to inequalities, unemployment and how to manage the public sector.

On the other hand, the need for intervention does not say anything about the extent to which, and in what way, interventions must be made as a result. They depend on the purpose of an intervention, but also how the goal can be achieved in the best and cheapest way.

REFERENCES

Bartlett, Will, and Julian Le Grand. 1993. "The Theory of Quasi-Markets." In *Quasi-Markets and Social Policy*, 13–34. London: Palgrave Macmillan.

Blanchard, Olivier, Alvaro Leandro, and Jeromin Zettelmeyer. 2021. "Redesigning EU Fiscal Rules: From Rules to Standards." *Economic Policy* 21:1.

Dursin, Wouter, Toon Benoot, Rudi Roose, and Bram Verschuere. 2021. "Choice and Opportunity on the Welfare Care Market: An Experimental Evaluation of Decision-Making in a Context of Individual Funding Policy." *Social Policy & Administration* 55 (7): 1276–92.

Eeckhout, Jan. 2020. "The Profit Paradox." In *The Profit Paradox*, 1st edn, 327. Princeton, NJ: Princeton University Press.

Forte, Francesco, and Alan T. Peacock. 1985. *Public Expenditure and Government Growth*. Oxford and New York: Blackwell.

Greve, B. 2010. *Can Choice in Welfare States Be Equitable? Challenges and Perspectives for the European Welfare States*. https://doi.org/10.1002/9781444324341.ch1.

Greve, B. 2021. *Multidimensional Inequalities. International Perspectives across Welfare States*. Berlin: De Gruyter.

Hirsch, Fred. 2013. *Social Limits to Growth*. Cambridge, MA: Harvard University Press (originally published 1976).

Hobbes, Thomas. 1980. *Leviathan (1651)* (originally published Glasgow 1974).

Keynes, John Maynard. 1936. *The General Theory of Employment, Interest, and Money*. London: Macmillan (originally published 1936).

Mueller, Dennis C. 1987. "The Growth of Government: A Public Choice Perspective." *Staff Papers* 34 (1): 115–49.

Musgrave, R. 1959. *The Theory of Public Finance*. New York: McGraw-Hill.

Musgrave, R., and P. Musgrave. 1989. *Public Finance in Theory and Practice*. New York: McGraw-Hill.

Nelson, Richard R. 1985. *An Evolutionary Theory of Economic Change*. Cambridge, MA: Harvard University Press.

Niskanen, William A. Jr 1971. *Bureaucracy and Representative Government*. New York: Aldine-Atherton.

OECD. 2021. *Main Findings from the 2020 Risks That Matter Survey*. https://doi.org/10.1787/b9e85cf5-en.

Pigou, Arthur Cecil. 1950. *The Economics of Welfare*. London: Palgrave Macmillan.

Smith, Adam. 1776. *An Inquiry into the Wealth of Nations. Book*. 1970 edn. London: J.M. Dent & Sons Ltd, Everymans Library. https://doi.org/10.7208/chicago/9780226763750.001.0001.

Stiglitz, J., and J. Rosengaard. 2015. *Economics of the Public Sector*. 4th edn. London: W.W. Norton & Company.

Susskind, Daniel. 2020. *A World without Work: Technology, Automation and How We Should Respond*. London: Penguin.

4.   Size of the public sector

4.1   INTRODUCTION

The size of the public sector influences the overall impact it has on societal and economic development in a given country. This chapter provides a particularly empirical description of the size and scope of the public sector in Europe.

The chapter shows how large the public sector is in relation to other parts of the economy, including how spending and income are measured and defined in national accounts. Does it matter, for example, whether the public sector itself produces or buys goods and services from private providers? Section 4.2 gives definitions of the public sector in the national accounts in order to show that understanding of the role of the public sector might be more blurred than at the outset if just looking into the publicly available data.

Comparative European data, as central for Section 4.3, are used to look at the differences in which types of spending on different policy fields are most emphasized in diverse countries, that is, to illustrate that there does not have to be a specific and common way of spending resources. This is because there have always been national differences in priorities, which is a continuing trend. It also opens the way for a discussion on how public expenditure can be perceived in some areas as investments in the future (e.g. research), or as elements that support labour supply (e.g. childcare). This is to illustrate the fact that public sector activities can have different effects and are justified on the basis of different ways of understanding the interaction between the public and private sectors. The book comes back to this topic in more detail in Chapter 11, also given that there can be short- as well as long-term impact on societal development.

Lastly, Section 4.4 sets out the conclusions.

4.2   PUBLIC SECTOR IN THE NATIONAL ACCOUNTS

It is one thing to argue that something is part of the public sector, but, at the same time, it is important in relation to cross-country comparison to be clear as to what is to be calculated as part of the public sector and what is to be understood as market-based activities. This is done in the national accounts systems, which almost 100 years ago was made more systematic, including at the time only a very limited number of definitions and rules for how to inform about the difference between the public and private sectors (Coyle 2015). In the 2008 edition of the *System of National Accounts* (SNA), the descriptions and definitions of the many and diverse sectors in a society are now 722 pages long and with a very detailed level of information and definitions of where different activities should be placed (see endnote 1), and rules and reasons therefore.

This applies in relation to both expenditure and revenue of the public sector, including that the public sector's activities range from direct provision of services (with or without user charges) to ownership of companies that provide services, for example within the supply of a number of produced goods (such as water, electricity, heating, railway tracks), because (as also described in Chapter 3) there will be areas where there would be no production without public sector intervention. However, this is not to say that part of it could not be provided by individual companies, such as even if the railroad tracks are publicly owned and maintained, then there could be competition between different providers of train services.

Central to the assessment of whether an item of expenditure should be included in the public or private sector in the national accounts is whether the public sector owns the company that provides the service or has a decisive influence on what companies do. It is thus defined as:

> A government unit usually has the authority to raise funds by collecting taxes or compulsory transfers from other institutional units. In order to satisfy the basic requirements of an institutional unit in the SNA, a government unit, whether at the level of the total economy, a region or a locality, must have funds of its own either raised by taxing other units or received as transfers from other government units and the authority to disburse some, or all, of such funds in the pursuit of its policy objectives. It must also be able to borrow funds on its own account.[1]

Further, a government unit will often have the option to ensure that it has income for its activities, without specifying how this is done. This can further include non-profit organizations that, with government support or on behalf of the government, carry out activities, which are then considered as part of public sector activities. Even private organizations where more than half of the activities are financed by the state can be considered as part of public sector activities.

The definition and measurement principles help in knowing the total public sector revenue, that is, not only taxes and duties, but also user fees.

Overall, it is further defined so that "the general government sector consists of institutional units which are non-market producers whose output is intended for individual and collective consumption, and are financed by units belonging to other sectors and institutional units principally engaged in the redistributions of national income and wealth".[2] Individual and collective consumption also refers to that part of public sector activities which can be referred to individual persons/families (such as care for children, long-term care and healthcare), whereas others can't (such as defence, foreign services, judiciary activities).

Given this common way of defining and measuring the public sector, international data can be used to compare across countries, albeit still with the need to know and be aware that the line between public and private provision is not straightforward and areas might overlap, and that there are consistent interdependencies among the sectors. Here, data from Eurostat are used as they define the public sector in the same way as in the SNA system, often labelled ESA.[3]

It is important to bear in mind that if the public sector regulates through legislation, it will not result in changes in what is registered in the public sector's economic consumption. Legislation on, for example, higher minimum wages is important for low-income groups who have a job, and, unlike income transfers, it is not registered as a public expense, but will instead be part of the employers' costs of production (Ozkan 2020). Likewise, if special subsidies are given to certain groups through less tax payment (tax expenditures) then it can be seen only indirectly by the fact that less tax revenue comes in than would otherwise have been the case (Morel, Touzet, and Zemmour 2018). In addition, there may be a difference between a country taxing or not taxing income transfers, which is important partly for the size of the total public income transfers and partly for measuring the tax burden. If they are taxed, both expenses and income will be higher in the national accounts without affecting the amount available to recipients. It is therefore important when comparing across countries to have knowledge of tax expenditures and rules for taxation, just as when looking at welfare states what types and opportunities there are in relation to occupational welfare (Greve 2018; Farnsworth 2019).

Therefore, it is important to know what detailed information is available in the statistics on public finances, but it is also important to keep an eye on elements that are not included or otherwise hidden in the statistics of the public sector activities.

4.3   DATA ON THE PUBLIC SECTOR – WHAT DO THEY SHOW?

The first key question is the size of the public sector in relation to the overall economy of a country. This is typically measured by calculating public consumption and total government expenditure as a share of gross domestic product (GDP). When looking at the development here, it needs to be taken into account that the share may be affected by both the development in expenditure and in the overall economic growth in a country. It is useful to look at both public consumption and public expenditure. Public consumption tells something about the consumption of resources for a sector in a country out of the total available resources, including that in richer nations larger public sectors tend to have a stronger impact on distribution. The total public expenditure, which also includes income transfers, is an illustration of the impact of the public sector not only on the consumption of resources, but also in relation to the allocation of economic resources. Naturally, the information given below should be interpreted with caution given the many and varied types of information that are available for a society are not reflected in the few data presented here.

A further, and also traditional, caveat is that the size of the government as a proportion of GDP is not only a question of the development within the public sector, but also the change in GDP. So that in times of strong economic growth the relative size might decline while there are still also in real prices more resources available, and in times of recession with a declining GDP, the proportion might increase, while in fact there are fewer real resources available. Still, it is also important to have an idea of the size of the government, and it is informative when looking into the development over a number of years.

Figure 4.1 shows the overall development for the European Union (EU) of total public sector spending as well as revenue.

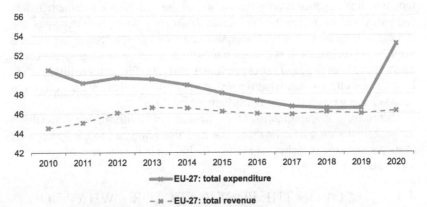

Note: Data extracted on 20 October 2021. Note that the y-axis is cut.
Source: Eurostat (gov_10a_main), https://ec.europa.eu/eurostat/statistics-explained/index .php?title=Government_finance_statistics#Government_revenue_and_expenditure, accessed 9 December 2021.

Figure 4.1   *Development of total expenditure and total revenue, 2010–20*

Figure 4.1 shows a number of issues, one being that expenditure can be influenced by external shocks such as the financial crisis in 2008–09, which explains the higher spending level in 2010, then gradually declining as a pro-portion of GDP when the economies were starting to grow again. The impact of COVID-19 can also clearly be witnessed by the sharp increase in spending in 2020.

Another issue is that in most years, with 2017 to 2019 as the exceptions, the size of spending has been larger than the revenue, implying a public sector deficit. The consequence hereof is returned to in a number of later chapters, including the growing levels of public sector debt in several countries, see albeit also Figure 4.4 below.

The development is not the same in all types of welfare states. This is depicted in Figure 4.2.

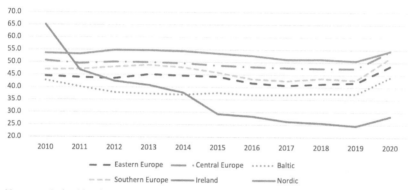

Note: Ireland is taken as a separate case given the very diverse development over the time-period.
Source: Own depiction based upon data from Eurostat (see Figure 4.1).

Figure 4.2   *Government expenditure as a percentage of GDP since 2010 in different welfare regimes*

Figure 4.2 indicates that the Nordic countries have the largest government spending, closely followed by Central Europe, and with the Baltic being the lowest spender. The data for Ireland is very high in 2010 in the aftermath of the financial crisis, with high spending on the bailout of the banking sector and then when this was reduced as one of the consequences of the high economic growth, the level declined dramatically. In all welfare regimes there has been an increase in 2020. Naturally, it is important to be aware that the overall level of spending does not inform about where and for what purposes the govern-ment is spending money. In order to know this, a more detailed analysis of the different parts of public sector spending is necessary. Part of this is reflected in Chapter 8, which looks into the largest spending areas of the public sector in most countries.

Figure 4.3 shows in more detail how different EU countries finance public sector spending, as those activities will need to be funded. Even if, in principle, the state could print money to finance activities, then in order to avoid longer-term problems and issues related hereto, as well as financing also having a role with regard to the overall economic activity in a society, one must be aware of how to finance and the consequences of different choices (to be returned to in Chapters 5 and 6).

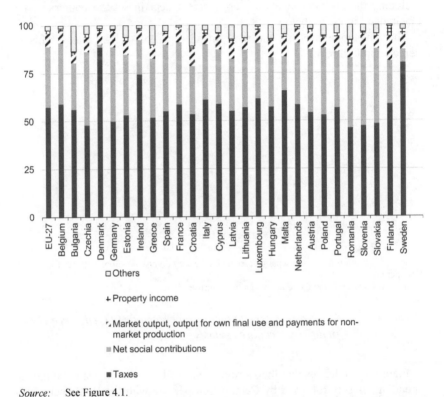

□ Others

＋ Property income

ʳ⸽ Market output, output for own final use and payments for non-market production

■ Net social contributions

■ Taxes

Source: See Figure 4.1.

Figure 4.3   Main components of government revenue, 2020 (% of total revenue)

Figure 4.3 is a clear indication that taxes and social security contributions are the main sources of income for the public sector in all EU countries, as is the case generally around the globe. The main difference is whether and how strong the focus is on income taxes or social security contributions. Income taxes are highest in the Nordic countries, whereas social security contributions are highest in a number of Eastern European countries (such as Slovenia, Slovakia and Romania). Besides that, all countries have a number of duties on different goods, including generally VAT on most goods and services. The way this is combined and the possible impact on societies' development are the focus in other chapters.

One issue, which is returned to later in the book, is the level of public sector deficit and debt, including how high this can be in a country and the possible short- as well as long-term consequences hereof.

Therefore, Figure 4.4 shows the level of public sector debt as a percentage of GDP.

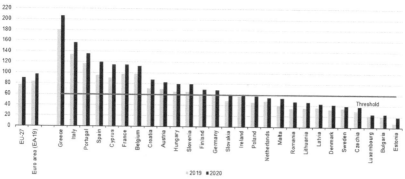

Note: Data extracted on 20 October 2021.
Source: See Figure 4.1.

Figure 4.4   General government debt, 2019 and 2020

The threshold in Figure 4.4 is set out in the rules related to the European Economic and Monetary Union in the EU's Stability and Growth Pact. Deficit shall not exceed 3 per cent (0.5 per cent for the structural deficit) of GDP and debt is at a maximum 60 per cent of GDP.[4] Whether this is the right level can be argued, and is discussed later in the book. Figure 4.4 shows the impact already in 2020 on the public sector debt as a consequence of the implemented stimulus packages in all countries in order to reduce the risk of strong increases in the level of unemployment related to the COVID-19 crisis, which has also implied that the debt has increased. Especially countries in Southern Europe have high levels of public sector debt, which might pose a problem at a later time, and high levels of debt might be more expensive to finance than low levels.

Governments can in general spend money on providing services (such as education) or transfer money to its citizens. There can be public sector investment as well as consumption. Formally, transfers are not calculated as the use of societal resources, whereas public consumption is. This is because transfers imply a redistribution from one group of citizens to another group of citizens. When citizens get the transfer they can use it for the purpose they so want, and when they spend the money this is counted as private consumption in the national accounts.

The choice between the use of income transfers and direct provision of goods can be due to a paternalistic approach, as some voters might prefer to pay for a specific use of the money (Barr 2020). It can also be because some persons might not be able, for different reasons, for example, to pay for their accommodation themselves, and thus even if the welfare state provides support to pay for the accommodation, they end up being at risk of becoming homeless unless the transfer goes directly to pay the landowners. Another example is lunch for children, which is argued in Chapter 3 to be a merit good. If not provided as food, the fear is that the children will not get the necessary food as the family might use the money, if provided as an income transfer, in another way. Persons' use of money for alcohol and drugs can also be a reason why some prefer to avoid direct cash benefits and, instead, use direct payments for food and accommodation. Such changes are thus done despite the fact that, in principle, the highest utility will be reached if the individual is able to choose from the available options in relation to his/her income constraints.

Thus, looking into public sector economics also implies a need to look into the way resources are distributed to different sectors, as well as whether this is done in-kind or in-cash, which is returned to in Chapter 8.

Spending can also have an influence on other parts of societies, including positive externalities, such as vaccination. It can also be social investment by, for example, increasing the level of human capital by education, as well as providing care for children, which opens the way to enable more people to have a job on the labour market. The social investment perspective is returned to in Chapter 10.

However, it is not only social investment that can be important, but as also argued in Chapter 3, there can be infrastructure investment which can best be done by the public sector in order to make it available for the general population and ensure a more efficient use hereof. This includes infrastructure such as roads, railway tracks, harbours, airports, bridges, and so on, albeit this does not always need to be done by the public sector.

Investment in basic research can also be an issue, given this will imply, if public, that all get access to it, in combination with the fact that not all basic research gets results. In total, a large amount of public sector investment can be important for private companies as it can support their production, while also that a large part of the investment in infrastructure, even if paid for by the public sector, is often done by private companies.

4.4 CONCLUSIONS

The public sector can be understood as the entity providing a number of non-market goods and services and where the state has a central role and also the ability and willingness to finance these. It can include a number of activities that, in principle, could be provided by the market, but as argued in Chapter 3, there can be a number of reasons for state intervention.

The size of the public sector is different across countries and welfare regimes, as is the way they are financed. Theoretically, it is not possible to decide what the best size of the public sector is, as this is influenced by the productivity in the public sector and the impact on the development of the society, including the possible consequences of the way in which the activities are financed. Furthermore, there can be different preferences among the voters of the combination of state and market activities. A central overall goal will be the most effective use and influence of societal resources, and the way in which this can be achieved.

NOTES

1. See https://unstats.un.org/unsd/nationalaccount/docs/SNA2008.pdf, p. 78, accessed 3 July 2021.
2. See https://ec.europa.eu/eurostat/statistics-explained/index.php?title=Governme nt_finance_statistics#Introduction, p. 11, accessed 3 July 2021.
3. See ibid.
4. See note 2.

REFERENCES

Barr, Nicholas. 2020. *The Economics of the Welfare State*. 6th edn. Oxford: Oxford University Press.

Coyle, Diane. 2015. *GDP: A Brief But Affectionate History – Revised and Expanded Edition*. Princeton, NJ: Princeton University Press.

Farnsworth, Kevin. 2019. "Occupational Welfare." In *The Routledge Handbook of the Welfare State*, edited by B. Greve, 2nd ed., 34–45. Oxon: Routledge.

Greve, B. 2018. "At the Heart of the Nordic Occupational Welfare Model: Occupational Welfare Trajectories in Sweden and Denmark." *Social Policy and Administration* 52 (2): 508–18. https://doi.org/10.1111/spol.12380.

Morel, Nathalie, Chloé Touzet, and Michaël Zemmour. 2018. "Fiscal Welfare in Europe: Why Should We Care and What Do We Know so Far?" *Journal of European Social Policy* 28 (5): 549–60. https://doi.org/10.1177/0958928718802553.

Ozkan, Umut Riza. 2020. "Mandatory Occupational Welfare: Severance Pay as an Unemployment Compensation Instrument." *Social Policy & Administration* 54 (1): 28–44.

5.   Taxation and impact on societies

The art of taxation consists in so plucking the goose as to obtain the largest amount of feathers with the least amount of hissing. (Jean Baptise Colbert, Finance Minister to Louis XIV of France)

5.1   INTRODUCTION

The chapter epigraph indicates a clearly difficult issue for those wanting to find ways to finance public sector spending. Often, those who have to pay would prefer to have others to pay instead of themselves.

Taxes and fees are defined by the fact that payment must be made to the state without the individual being able to have the right to any benefit, neither cash nor service, should there be a need for this. This is in contrast to, for example, user fees where there will be a right to specific services, such as childcare or healthcare.

Historically, taxes have played, and continue to do so, a central role in many and very different areas of a society. This applies, for example, in relation to issues of the possible impact on labour supply, saving, pollution and changes in the composition of consumption. This chapter presents and discusses how taxation might be carried out in order not only to finance public sector activities, but also to influence allocation, distribution and stabilization. This is the focus of Section 5.2.

In addition, there may be differences in the distributional effects of using different taxes and duties, while there must be a willingness to pay the necessary taxes and duties in order to finance the public sector, and this might be influenced by the distributional impact, which is the core of Section 5.3. These possible conflicts and their impact on societies' development are discussed, including who in fact pays the different taxes and duties (the tax incidence). Exemptions in the tax systems (see also later on tax expenditures) can be a way of supporting or reducing payments for certain groups.

This is followed in Section 5.4 by a presentation of taxation's possible impact on labour supply and savings, as this has been one of the central discussions in several welfare states as to whether and, if so, how the tax system distorts the development of societies. Section 5.5 briefly presents the reasons why taxation can be an instrument related to environmental global challenges. Taxation is part of fiscal policy, but the impact of different types of fiscal policy is first returned to in Chapter 6, including more specifically on the overall tax structure, as well as the possible restrictions on national taxation by globalization in Chapter 10.

Section 5.6 concludes the chapter.

5.2 ALLOCATION, DISTRIBUTION AND STABILIZATION

There has historically been an abundant number of different ways for rulers to ensure they had the necessary financing of their activities, including war. In Box 5.1, an extract from a book shows that most of the historical challenges in financing the public sector are, in many ways, still the same today. Thus, the impact of taxes on behaviour as well as their possible impact on allocation, distribution and stabilization has been part of societal development, as well as the imagination and ability to find a variety of different ways to ensure revenue.

BOX 5.1 A HISTORICAL EXAMPLE OF TAXATION AND BEHAVIORAL CHANGE

This is the tale of the window tax, imposed in Britain from 1697 to 1851. At first blush, taxing windows may seem anachronistic or just plain folly. But it was actually pretty clever.

The problem faced by the government of the time was to find a tax based on something that: increased with wealth (for fairness); was easily verified (to avoid disputes); and – being intended to replace a tax on hearths (that is fireplace), much hated for requiring inspectors to check insides the property ... (pp. 19–20)

Because people preferred to both keep their windows and pay less tax, the response to the window tax, as with most taxes, was largely a story of evasion and avoidance, dispute, and legislative change trying to clarify the tax rules about what was and was not subject to tax. (p. 21)

Source: Keen and Slemrod (2021).

As the quote indicates, attempts to evade and avoid taxes and duties have been part of the history of taxation, and continue to this day. Thus, the public sector deficit would, in most countries, be reduced if the size of tax evasion and the hidden economy could be reduced, implying that there is, presumably, a constant need for ensuring compliance with the tax rules.

The historical examples further illustrate that when choosing different taxes and duties, there will easily be some resistance, although there may be different reasons for this, such as control of behaviour or the feeling that it is not a fair form of taxation. This does not mean that it is theoretically possible to determine what a fair form of taxation is, as it will depend on normative considerations. But it shows that taxation can be difficult to implement and, therefore, as also pointed out historically by Musgrave and Musgrave (1989), "hidden" taxes are often more acceptable than taxes that can be more easily seen. For example, in most countries prices in shops are shown including the Value Added Tax (VAT), thus consumers react to the price, not the tax imposed on the good unless (see discussions later) this changes. Taken together, Musgrave and Musgrave pointed out that a good tax structure must have the following elements:

(a)   Sufficient revenue
(b)   Fair distribution of the taxes and duties levied
(c)   Minimization of distortions
(d)   Opportunity to use to stabilize the economy
(e)   Fair and open administrative system
(f)   Simple and inexpensive to administer.

Others have similar elements and requirements for the tax structure, such as: economic efficiency, administrative simplicity, flexibility, political responsiveness and fairness (Stiglitz and Rosengaard 2015).

These desires for a good tax structure are difficult to fulfil at one and the same time, and as a consequence there will be some choices to be made which also help to explain that taxes and duties often, and periodically, change, as do the rules for what is taxed and on what criteria, and the level of taxation. Furthermore, taxes and duties can be combined with other forms of public regulations (such as legal rules).

At the same time, taxes and duties can, in principle, be introduced everywhere in the economic cycle – again, with a focus on how to ensure an overall good tax structure and how it can be used to influence society's development, especially with a focus on their impact on allocation, distribution and stabilization. It also applies here that it is not a given fact that what is good for the allocation of resources needs to have the desired distributional effects.

The following is a brief description of two of the three functions in relation to taxation (see also Chapter 2 for a more detailed description of these aims), and see, in relation to distribution, Section 5.3.

The allocation of resources (land, labour and capital) aims to ensure its most optimal use, but may also aim to change consumption in what is seen as a more desired combination of societal consumption. Thus increases in duties might imply less consumption, but will also influence the production (whether for a national or international company of the product). Thus it may be, for example, to reduce the number of people who smoke by imposing taxes on cigarettes, and so on. Influencing the allocation can, as just one example, also have the purpose of helping to reduce the climate impact of production and consumption. This can be done, for example, through a tax on CO_2. The impact depends on the elasticity of the demand of the goods (see Figure 5.1, and later Figure 5.2).

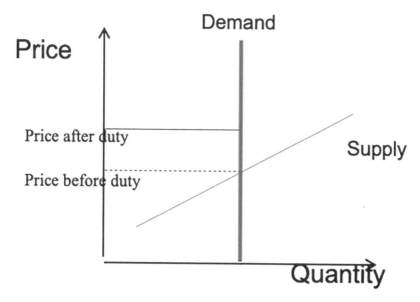

Figure 5.1   *Impact of a duty on necessary goods*

Figure 5.1 is an indication of what the impact will be on goods which are necessary (and therefore there is no change in quantity of demand when imposing a duty) such as water, electricity and heating, and also as there are only limited options to change to other types of supply. This is not to argue that some effect might not be there, but to indicate the possibility that only the price will change not the quantity. Further, this implies a risk that low-income groups will be influenced to a stronger extent as a higher proportion of their income is spent on these goods than higher-income groups. This can imply a need for the compensation of low-income groups when, for example, imposing environmental duties.

Historically, and also as a result of the negative externalities (cf. Chapter 3), such as an impact on the environment, it has been argued that when the market does not include an effect on the environment in the price, other instruments must be used to achieve this goal, that is, through taxes, but also, in principle, other forms of regulation, so that the polluter will have to pay.

The impact on societal economic development (the stabilization task) aims to ensure economic development without excessive fluctuations in both upward and downward directions. Therefore, as discussed in more detail in Chapter 6, it may be possible to adjust economic activity by changing the overall level of taxes and duties, including the composition of taxation, in order to even out cyclical fluctuations in economies. There will be some who believe that the market should be able to regulate without public intervention. Knowledge of how different types of interventions work is therefore an important element in deciding whether or not there should be interventions in the current economic situation. Nevertheless, there is the option for the public sector to influence, which is returned to in Section 6.2 with a discussion on automatic stabilizers and active fiscal policy interventions.

It is constantly important to be aware that using an instrument to achieve one aim might have a negative impact on another aim. Just to give one illustration, duties on cigarettes might help in improving the allocation of resources in a healthier direction; however, given that people with low incomes more often smoke, higher duties can have a negative impact on the distribution and the risk of increased cross-border trade, for example, to seek out lower-duty regimes. How to balance these issues is, at the end of the day, a political, not an economic, issue, albeit economics might help in estimating the cost on a number of issues by using different decisions. Still, it is also important to know what the impact on the economic distribution is, which is the focus of the next section.

5.3   HOW DO DIFFERENT INSTRUMENTS INFLUENCE INEQUALITY?

As the example in the previous section indicates, it is not easy to determine the distributive effect of different taxes and duties on the basis of a tax rate. There will be a number of factors that need to be investigated in order for the effect to be assessed.

In the following, this is exemplified by first looking at the three theoretical effects income taxes may have, and then at how different elements can affect this.

A distinction can be made between progressive, proportional and regressive taxes. In the case of progressive taxes, people with higher incomes pay relatively more (a higher share of the income) in tax than people with lower incomes, typically by taxing part of the income above a threshold at a higher tax rate. With a proportional income tax, the tax rate is the same for all incomes and thus basically the same (share of income) for everyone, whereas a regressive tax is relatively higher for people with lower incomes. This means that progressive taxes can contribute to a more equal distribution of income after tax than before tax, while at the same time the total distributional effect depends on what the tax revenue is used for, and also, in order that taxation is

Table 5.1   *Illustrative example of the impact of tax threshold and level of taxation for individuals*

Yearly income	Tax threshold (general personal allowance) 5000, tax rate 25%	Relative percentages
5000	(5000–5000)*0.25 = 0	0
20 000	(20 000–5000)*0.25 = 3750	3750/20 000 =18.75
50 000	(50 000–5000)*0.25 = 11,250	11 250/50 000 = 22.5

Note: These figures are purely to illustrate the impact of a general personal allowance and thus neither tax rate nor income level is from any specific country.

socially acceptable (Diamond and Saez 2011), that there are good reasons for progressive income taxes. A proportional tax does not redistribute, whereas a regressive tax increases economic inequality.

However, this can be affected by other elements of the tax system. Even a proportional tax can affect the distribution of disposable income in a more equal direction. This applies if there is a lower limit that must be exceeded before income tax must be paid. For example, in the case of an income during a year where the first 5000 Euro is not taxed by a proportional income tax, people with higher incomes will pay relatively more in tax (cf. the example above in Table 5.1) with a proportional tax of 25 per cent.

As can be seen from Table 5.1, the relative taxation varies with the proportional tax rate of 25 per cent between 0 per cent and 22.5 per cent, and for very high incomes it will be close to 25 per cent. The table also shows that the important issue when judging a tax system is not the absolute tax rate or the amount to be paid, but the relative tax rate in the last column.

It is often also more important to look into the marginal tax rate as this informs about what is due to be paid from the last earned income, which is returned to in Section 5.4.

The same applies for VAT. Even if it looks like everyone is paying the same, it is regressive because low-income earners spend a higher proportion of their income on consumption, whereas persons with higher income have a higher level of saving. If one wants to ensure that those best able to pay taxes and duties pay more than other persons, then one needs also to know something about the composition of consumption patterns when using duties so that one can impose a duty on what is labelled luxury goods.

In many countries, goods such as perfume, for example, are seen as luxury goods. Although there may also be foods that can be seen as luxury goods, it can often be more difficult to make a separate tax on these, as it can be difficult to administer compared with the requirements for what constitutes a good tax structure.

There is also an analytical problem related to the fact that it is not certain that the person who must immediately pay a tax/duty, for example, is also the one who will pay. It depends on whether the tax can be passed on to others to pay these, also referred to as the tax incidence. Overall, the tax incidence depends on how elastic both demand and supply are. The elasticity is defined as the percentage change in consumption/production as a consequence of a percentage change in the price of the good. This thus says something about how much can and will be produced/consumed when there are changes in prices as a result of, for example, changes in taxes. Completely inelastic demand means that the price increases with the size of the tax, and in the case of inelastic supply, the price does not change as a result of imposing a duty. Completely elastic demand means that the consumption of the product will change fully as a result of the duty, and conversely with a full elastic supply, the price will increase by the amount of the tax. This will therefore have consequences for who pays the tax in the end. However, there is often a mix of who pays, so it will often be both producer and consumer who are affected, with consumers having to pay more and buy less and producers producing less than before a tax was introduced.

This can be summed up as follows:

(1)   Completely elastic demand means it is the manufacturer who pays
(2)   If the supply is completely inelastic, the manufacturer pays the tax
(3)   If the supply is completely elastic, then consumers pay all taxes
(4)   If the demand is inelastic, then the consumer pays the whole tax
(5)   In all other situations, the incidence depends on both demand and supply elasticity of who actually pays taxes.

This is illustrated in Figure 5.2 to indicate that whether one imposes a tax on buyers or producers the outcome will be the same related to the change in price of the good and the quantity consumed. In both cases prices for the consumers increase to p^i and the price received by producers is reduced to p^{ii}, and the quantity sold at the market reduced to q^1.

Figure 5.2 also indicates that there will always be a need for an empirical analysis to be able to concretely determine who pays a new tax. This can be difficult, as there is not always precise information about how individuals will react to changes in the price, including that since people have different preferences, average changes in preferences will have to be found, and this is not simple.

There may also be taxes on land and real estate, as there may be an interest in taxing non-mobile tax sources, as it will be a more secure revenue for the states (cf. more in Chapter 9). There can also be other taxes on, for example, electricity, water and heat, which are consumables that are greatly affected by

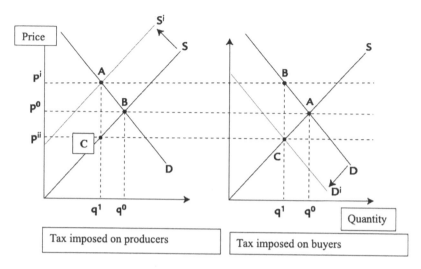

Figure 5.2   The impact of imposing a duty and who pays

where people are located. At the same time, taxes on land and real estate can be seen as fair taxes in the sense that there is typically a connection between one's housing consumption and one's income. Despite this, today there is only a more limited use of it in most countries, for example, due to the fact that if it is a very visible taxation many voters do not like it. It is more visible, for example, than VAT, as it must be paid directly by the individual, whereas VAT is included in the price of the goods, and thus is not to the same extent seen as a visible tax. The economic arguments for taxes on land and houses are that, in principle, there shall not be a difference between placing money in different kinds of capital (such as stocks and bonds) and housing, as the "income" of owning a house is that there is no rent to pay. Therefore, theoretically, the taxation of housing should be at the level of the real interest in societies.

Subsidies for goods and services can, in principle, have the same effects, so that even if, for example, public subsidies are given for housing consumption, it is not certain that it is the recipient who has the full benefit of the subsidy. It is theoretically possible that a new subsidy reducing the cost for a property owner benefits only the owner of a rental property, unless other rules prevent this, who can then profit from renting out the dwelling at the same price as before the subsidy. Similarly, if subsidies are given for other products, there is a need to investigate who finally benefits financially from a subsidy, that is, the producer or the buyer, as in the situation with adding a tax.

There will be a similar need for empirical analysis in almost all areas of the tax system. To illustrate, even if there is, for example, a progressive scale for the payment of income tax, then there may be tax expenditures (Musgrave 1981; Barrios et al. 2019; Sinfield 2019), which will have an impact on the overall distributional effect. Tax expenditures typically have a negative effect on the economic distribution, and they might therefore be able to reduce the progressive effect of income taxes. They are labelled tax expenditures because the ability to make deductions in what to pay reduces the revenue for welfare states. Tax expenditures are defined as a departure from the generally accepted or benchmark structure implying a favourable tax treatment of some groups in a society. Thus when looking into the public sector economy, it is important to look at not only tax rates, but also other parts of the tax system, including different kinds of tax relief.

Naturally, one needs to be aware that not only do taxes have an impact on distribution, but also that access to public services and income transfers are important elements. For example, it can be the case that a 1 per cent increase in social transfers is argued to reduce inequality by 0.5 per cent (d'Agostino, Pieroni, and Scarlato 2020), so that even if the taxation does not by itself (as it often does) influence the degree of inequality, then the way the money is spent can have an impact.

5.4   TAXES' IMPACT ON LABOUR SUPPLY AND SAVING

It is often discussed whether tax can have an impact on how much the individual will work, for example, because the quantity of labour might have an impact on overall production, but also because there is a demographic development heading towards fewer people being of working age. It is especially the marginal income tax that is often discussed. The logic is that income tax has an impact on how much we want to work compared to a situation without the tax. However, it is important to be aware that it is the combined marginal change in disposable income that is of interest, that is, not only what the income tax is on the last earned income, but also whether there is an impact on the receipt of various social benefits, which is often dependent on income (cf. also Chapter 8). User charges, for example, payment for day-care, can also influence the combined marginal change in disposable income. Or more simply, what the disposable income is before and after tax and possible phasing out of social benefits. Still, one will need to have income from taxes and duties to finance societal activities, and it is this balance which needs to be achieved.

An analytical problem is that it is compared to a situation where there is no tax, but given that as mentioned earlier in the chapter, taxes and duties have always been needed to finance society, then it is not necessarily the best basis for comparison, although it does not change the fact that it is important to know the positive effects of different types of taxes and duties, and thus be able to choose the combination that gives the fewest distortions when influencing the individual's behaviour.

Theoretically, a distinction is made between an income and a substitution effect. This is illustrated in Figure 5.3.

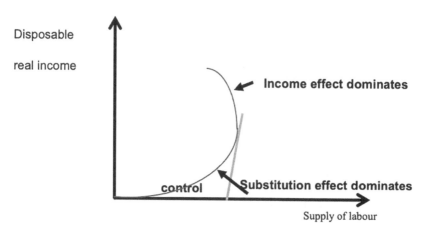

Figure 5.3   Impact on labour supply by change in disposable real income

The income effect will mean that if lowering the income tax, we will work less as we can have the same disposable income even if we work less, and vice versa if the income tax increases. The substitution effect is that we balance how much we want to work and how much time we have for leisure. If the tax is increased, we will work less because it is then perceived as less attractive to work, and vice versa if it is lowered. It is an empirical question which of the two effects is greater. There is often assumed to be a higher elasticity for high-income earners than for low-income earners, implying that high-income earners will work more if the marginal income tax is lowered. The difference is witnessed in Figure 5.3 by the backward sloping curve, so that a higher disposable income can, on average, imply a reduction in the labour supply from persons having such levels of income. This is, at the same time, questionable given that there is decreasing marginal utility of extra income, so that even if working more the extra benefit of the income will have less value for those already having a high income than for those with a low income.

Empirically, it can be difficult to calculate the elasticity of labour supply, partly because not all people have the same preferences, and partly because there are a number of other factors that have an impact on the labour supply. This applies, for example, to the change in demand for labour, but also to the fact that it is not necessarily possible for a person to freely change working hours depending on changes in the tax system, as many persons will and may be faced with a choice to work or not to work. In addition, in a number of countries, various forms of special tax deductions for people in the labour market (earned income tax credits) have been introduced, which also influence the choice between work and leisure. The impact might also be stronger in relation to the self-employed as it is easier for them to have the option to increase or decrease the number of hours they will work compared to people who are employed (see Saez, Slemrod, and Giertz 2012, who also argued that, empirically, this is very difficult to estimate from a short- as well as a long-term perspective). This also includes that the effect depends on many dimensions of the tax system, and that it might be different between men and women, including variations in national social security systems.

In addition, in most western countries, both men and women are in the labour market, and there may also be social elements in having a job. The work–family life balance might thus also influence the labour supply.

Calculations are also complicated by the fact that they can have different effects depending on whether it is the bottom tax rate or the top tax rate that changes and where the threshold for paying the top income tax is. It is therefore difficult to assess whether or not it has an effect, it can vary over time, but also from country to country, and from family to family. Thus, even if one member of a family works more, another member might work less as this then might improve the work–life balance. When it can vary over time, it is also because, historically, working hours have fallen due to countries becoming richer, as part of the increasing wealth is taken out in the form of more leisure time.

Impacts can also depend on what the alternative to having a job is, and therefore the connection to, for example, the possibility of having public income transfers and their size influence this. This is indicated in Figure 5.3 by the control in the bottom when receiving benefits (see also more in Chapter 8 on possible conditions attached to receiving benefits). Here, however, it is the case that given public services in case of unemployment are time-limited, and often with requirements for activation, and so on, the effect on the labour supply of this in most countries must be assumed to be limited. Again, there will be a need for constant analysis of what the best combination of different taxes and duties will be and how to minimize possible types of distortions of behaviour.

Taxes on capital income can, in principle, influence the level of savings, so that a high level of taxes on dividends and interest will, theoretically, reduce the overall level of saving. How to combine an ambition to tax those with the highest income and wealth with the possible impact on the level of saving is an open question.

5.5 GREEN TAXES

The pressure on the environment is largely (as already indicated in Chapter 3) a consequence of market failure, as the costs of polluting the environment are not included in the prices of the goods and services that consumers buy, and thus the marginal cost and marginal utility are not equal to each other, which is a prerequisite for the market to function optimally. This is because the prices today of goods and services do not reflect the societal economic costs of production.

There are negative externalities associated with a wide range of activities in modern societies in terms of impact on the environment. They also have the problem that a country cannot necessarily do things alone, and that taxes that are supposed to reduce the environmental impact can risk moving production to a country without the same types and level of taxation.

Conversely, if no taxation is implemented, there may be significant risks to both national and global impacts on the environment. We thus here have an issue of not only national market failures, but also global market failures, implying that international collaboration on the issue is important.

Similarly, there may be an issue in relation to inequality, as environmental taxes tend to be regressive. But this could be compensated for in another way, if desired by decision makers, for example, through lowering of other taxes or by subsidies for low-income families.

Overall, it does not change the fact that taxes and duties will be a possible instrument that will and can effectively reduce the level of emissions that negatively affect the environment. As also stated in the section on externalities, it is theoretically also possible to regulate via legislation, although it may be difficult to set a precise limit for this, just as this will also have to be controlled. The sale of rights to pollute, which also exists today, would theoretically also be an option (Nordhaus 2021); Nordhaus also argues that for the US a carbon tax of 40 US$ per ton would be equivalent to the marginal negative impact on society. There is, naturally, a need to estimate this, including whether it will be sufficient to reduce pollution to such an extent that the ambition of reducing the increase in global temperature can be reached. It goes without saying that instead of taxation one might use legal regulation, although a tax seems simpler to implement, and can at the same time imply a revenue for societies. Or, as argued, that one "can apply the Goldilocks principle: Regulation should be neither too hot, nor too cold, but just right. In other words, it is necessary to find the appropriate balance between no regulation, and draconian regulation" (Nordhaus 2021, 307).

Using a tax on CO_2 and other greenhouse gas emissions will imply that prices for consumers will indicate which product has the highest emissions (as they will be taxed at a higher rate) and this will also be the case for producers who might then change to new ways of producing the good. This will further make it attractive to invest in new types of production with a lower impact on emissions, and lastly it is a relatively simple way to inform on the consequences of different levels of emission. A possible disadvantage can be that it influences the competitiveness if a country does it alone, so again international agreement would be important. As would it be good that the taxes are gradually increased and that consumers and producers know this will be the case, as they will then gradually change the consumption and production preferences. Countries being the first to introduce increases might even, at the same time, gain competitiveness by the development of new products with a lower impact on the environment.

5.6   CONCLUSIONS

There are many and varied issues when it comes to financing the activities of the public sector, while at the same time ensuring that there is sufficient revenue. Furthermore, efforts must be made to ensure the overall best effects on society's economic development when using different kinds of taxes and duties.

There will usually be both expected and unexpected effects of introducing, changing or removing taxes and duties. How this affects allocation, distribution and stabilization are key issues that must be constantly weighed against each other, and this can best be assessed empirically. This also implies that in order to reach specific goals, a combination of different taxes and duties needs to be used, as well as in combination with how the public sector spends its money.

Still, taxes and duties are important instruments that can be used to influence societal development – whether it is the ability to finance the welfare state, to influence the business cycle, to work, to save or to reduce pollution. Therefore, taxation has historically been an important part of societies' development, and will presumably continue to be so, implying a constant need to analyse and understand how taxation works in a changing society.

REFERENCES

Barrios, Salvador, Flavia Coda Moscarola, Francesco Figari, Luca Gandullia, and Sara Riscado. 2019. "The Fiscal and Equity Impact of Social Tax Expenditures in the EU." *Journal of European Social Policy* 30 (3): 355–69.
d'Agostino, Giorgio, Luca Pieroni, and Margherita Scarlato. 2020. "Social Transfers and Income Inequality in OECD Countries." *Structural Change and Economic Dynamics* 52: 313–27.

Diamond, Peter, and Emmanuel Saez. 2011. "The Case for a Progressive Tax: From Basic Research to Policy Recommendations." *Journal of Economic Perspectives* 25 (4): 165–90.

Keen, Michael, and Joel Slemrod. 2021. *Rebellion, Rascals, and Revenue. Tax Follies and Wisdon through the Ages.* Princeton, NJ: Princeton University Press.

Musgrave, R. 1981. "Leviathan Cometh – or Does He?." In *Tax and Expenditure Limitations*, edited by H. Ladd and N. Tideman. Washington, DC: Urban Institute.

Musgrave, R., and P. Musgrave 1989. *Public Finance in Theory and Practice.* New York: McGraw-Hill.

Nordhaus, William D. 2021. *The Spirit of Green: The Economics of Collisions and Contagions in a Crowded World.* Princeton, NJ: Princeton University Press.

Saez, Emmanuel, Joel Slemrod, and Seth H. Giertz. 2012. "The Elasticity of Taxable Income with Respect to Marginal Tax Rates: A Critical Review." *Journal of Economic Literature* 50 (1): 3–50.

Sinfield, A. 2019. "Fiscal Welfare." In *The Routledge Handbook of the Welfare State*, edited by B. Greve, 2nd edn, 23–33. Oxon: Routledge.

Stiglitz, J., and J. Rosengaard. 2015. *Economics of the Public Sector.* 4th edn. London: W.W. Norton & Company.

6.   Fiscal policy – what works what does not work

6.1   INTRODUCTION

Fiscal policy is a key instrument for the public sector to influence societal economic development, as already indicated in Chapter 2 with the focus on allocation, distribution and stabilization. This chapter looks at both automatic stabilizers and deliberate changes (active fiscal policy) in public expenditure and/or revenue that can have an economic impact. The multiplier effect is explained, including that empirical analysis is important in order to know the exact magnitude of the various effects. Thus, it can also be discussed which types of intervention can have the best effect, which can also be influenced by what there is a political desire to achieve, and which instruments can be the most effective instruments to use given a specific aim of the intervention. The chapter also looks at how this can play together with the development of the business cycle and employment in a society.

Thus, the chapter starts in Section 6.2 by distinguishing the difference between automatic stabilizers and active fiscal policy, including how they work and in what situations the different types of interventions are made.

Section 6.3 describes and explains what fiscal multipliers are in order to have an idea of what will be the most effective types of intervention in the ongoing economic conditions and influenced by the preferences of policy makers.

Section 6.4 then discusses changes in the tax structure over time, as well as the interrelation between fiscal policy and overall economic development, before Section 6.5 concludes the chapter.

6.2   AUTOMATIC STABILIZERS AND ACTIVE FISCAL POLICY

A distinction can be made between automatic stabilizers and discretionary interventions in a society's economy.

An automatic stabilizer affects the economic development in a country without the need to make changes in rules and/or rates when collecting taxes and duties or spending public money. To exemplify, all developed countries have value added taxes (VAT), albeit with different levels and not necessarily on all goods and services. Food and clothes for children are often exempted or with a very low rate. Still, as an example, a country having a VAT rate of 25 per cent implies that if people due to higher economic activity buy more goods or services, then automatically more revenue comes into the public sector, and conversely, if people buy fewer goods, less money comes in. Similarly, with the taxation of income from greater economic activity and more people in work, the revenue of the public sector increases completely automatically; and, conversely, if the economic activity becomes smaller, so less money comes in. Automatic stabilizers are not just taxes and duties, but also include public sector spending, such as unemployment benefit and other income transfers. These transfers enable those, for example, made redundant in times of economic crisis to continue to have at least some income to spend and thereby they reduce the possible change in overall economic consumption and the impact of changes in businesses, so that the economic development is smoother.

This means that the public sector automatically influences in a number of ways the overall economic activity of a society without new decisions having to be made. This is also an indication that the public sector has an important ability to regulate the overall economic activity in a society, given that automatic stabilizers function immediately, whereas political decisions might take time, and even first be decided when there has again been a change in the overall economic activity with the risk that changes are then not what is needed in the overall economic activity.

In contrast, there are discretionary changes (active fiscal policy), such as higher/lower taxes on some items, or changes in taxation of wages or business income. The discretionary changes may be intended to reduce economic activity (through higher taxes and duties) or increase economic activity (through lower taxes and duties), but may also (as described in Chapter 5) be intended to influence consumption in certain directions, for example, less smoking and alcohol consumption. Active fiscal policy has, also historically, been seen as an important way to influence economic activity. Active fiscal policy can also be changes in the public sector spending as this also can have an impact on the number of jobs, and so on. Many countries use, for example, in times of economic crisis, more money on construction as this effectively increases employment and thereby the demand for other goods and services. The logic is, further, that when employment increases and people are then able to buy goods and services, those getting this income will also have money to spend. This is what is behind what is labelled fiscal multipliers. It is like rings spreading outwards in water after a stone is dropped into it.

It can be indicated in the following way:

Increase in taxes and ⇨ Higher public sector ⇨ Decrease in ⇨ Lower public sector revenue and higher
duties   revenue   employment   expenditure on unemployment benefit

This will then continue in a number of rounds with a gradually less strong impact, but will still ensure a more stable development than without these automatic stabilizers. Starting with lower taxes and duties will have the opposite impact of what is shown.

Overall, the largest impact when making an active fiscal intervention on economic growth and employment is direct employment in the public sector, followed by construction work. The reason why is because it causes direct employment, whereas, for example, a lowering of VAT has a lesser impact due to that this works through change in consumption, and besides that all consumption is not nationally produced implying that part of the change in employment will be in foreign countries. This is not to neglect the fact that if many countries at the same time ensure a fiscal expansion in order to increase higher levels of employment, then this will have a stronger impact on the level of employment also in other countries given the high degree of interconnectedness across countries. The impact is stronger across countries having closer economic relations with each other in the form of imports and exports.

6.3   FISCAL MULTIPLIERS – WHEN AND HOW TO USE THEM?

When changes are to be made to taxes and duties, or public expenditure, then it is necessary to know what the derived effects are, that is, not only changes in revenue that can have an influence on the public budget surplus or deficit as well as debt are of interest. But also, how changes will affect the economic distribution, the overall economic activity (including growth), the allocation of resources between areas, and the impact on the current account of the balance of payments. The impacts on economic activity are looked into in Section 6.4. Thus, as already pointed out in Section 6.2, the impact of stabilizers and active fiscal policy are examples that there will be a number of effects from changes in spending and/or taxes and duties in the public sector on the overall societal development.

A balanced budget multiplier (and, at the same time, increases in public sector expenditure and taxes) implies a stimulation of the overall economic activity, given that public sector spending has a stronger impact on economic activities and employment than taxes and duties, especially on taxes on higher-income groups as they have a higher savings rate than other income groups in society. The size hereof depends on national circumstances and how large the changes in spending and taxes and duties are, and the more specific way the changes are done. Direct employment in the public sector thus implies more jobs than if subsidies are given to companies or income transfers to citizens. A central question is whether there is the willingness to pay more taxes and duties. If, on the other hand, one combines lower taxes and duties with lower public sector spending, this might have a negative multiplier impact on economic activities as well as on employment/unemployment.

From an overall economic societal point of view, if the public sector by the use of fiscal multipliers helps in reducing the level of unemployment, this can be positive. This is because the production by each person increases societies' economic position, and as a contrast the possible production by an unemployed person can't be saved for a later time, so unemployment implies the waste of a productive factor in a society.

Therefore, depending on the macroeconomic situation, there can be a need for public sector intervention to reduce or increase economic activity in a particular society. Given, also, that the impact of fiscal policy intervention might be higher in an economic downturn, in principle, this might also reduce public sector debt besides influencing the level of unemployment (Constâncio 2020).

In addition to the direct effects of implementing an active fiscal policy, there may also be a possibility of what can be described as dynamic effects, also implying that one can't just look at the short-term impact when making a decision, but must be aware of longer-term issues. Employing more people in the public sector might in the short run reduce unemployment, but might be dependent on economic development in the longer run, implying less labour for the private sector. This implies that investment in infrastructure might be better as this combines higher levels of employment in the short run with better production and living conditions in the long run.

This further means that if (cf. also Chapter 11) there are better care options for caring for children and others, then this may affect the possibility of changes in the labour supply. This applies to more education, which can create opportunities for new and other types of jobs than previously, just as investments in infrastructure can contribute to having a higher economic activity than would otherwise be possible. Methodologically, there are issues in measuring these dynamic impacts, as well as those related to the impact on the labour supply by changes in the tax system (see Chapter 5). Nevertheless, it can be important to have an idea about the full impact, which is more than just the direct impact of changes in the various subsections of the public spending have on societal development.

When trying to estimate the effects of fiscal policy interventions, there are three elements that are included:

(1)   Immediate effects
(2)   Derived effects
(3)   Behavioural changes.

The immediate effects are those that are directly a consequence of a decision, for example, to spend a billion Euro in one area or to lower taxes and fees by one billion Euro. However, when spending is increased the effects will be different depending on whether it is on service or income transfers. Still, higher economic activities mean that some people may get a job instead of being unemployed. Fewer people unemployed reduces expenses and increases other tax revenues. If changes in expenditure or revenue have an impact on citizens' behaviour, it may increase or decrease the overall economic impact of a decision on the public sector economy as well as society in general. For example, if changes increase/decrease labour supply or change consumption of some goods with high taxes to low taxes. The latter is, theoretically, whether it was what was wanted or not. Increased taxes on tobacco for the purpose of reducing smoking can probably make someone quit smoking, and thus consumption can shift from high- to low-taxed goods.

Where it is relatively certain what the immediate effects are, as it is a decided amount, and where the derived effects can often be calculated fairly predictably from historical data, it is considerably more difficult to have reliable knowledge about the influence on behaviour. It may therefore also be necessary to present alternative estimates for the total effects on public expenditure and revenue, but also the distribution, as well as, for example, the labour supply. Although there are theoretical expectations for a change, it will be necessary to have empirical studies to create better knowledge about changes, in order to also have a more precise assumption of the overall societal impact. There might be national differences so, for example, it will be different in the UK and in Greece. In addition to the effects mentioned, there may be reasons to consider the consequences of inflation, economic growth and developments in the current account of the balance of payments.

6.4   FISCAL POLICY AND ECONOMIC DEVELOPMENT

Decisions on fiscal policy changes do not take place in a vacuum. They are related to the total economic activity, as indicated in the previous section, just as the choice of instruments depends on how taxes and duties are already levied. Therefore, in this section there is information on the tax structure of a number of countries in Europe. The countries are chosen to cover Northern, Southern, Eastern and Western Europe and thus countries with different historical traditions in a number of areas. This is shown in Figure 6.1.[1]

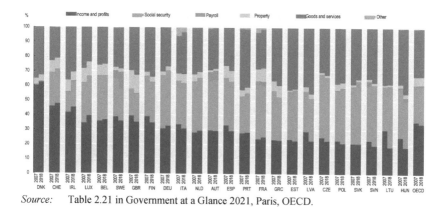

Source: Table 2.21 in Government at a Glance 2021, Paris, OECD.

Figure 6.1   *Breakdown of tax revenues as a percentage of total taxation, 2007 and 2018*

Figure 6.1 shows that there are large variations in the structure of taxation. Denmark has the highest percentage of public sector income from income taxation, the Czech Republic from social security contributions and Estonia from duties on goods and services. There have only been limited changes since 2008 in the way countries combine the use of various types of instruments in which they collect taxes and duties. Figure 6.1 also indicates that income taxes, social security contributions and duties on goods and services are the central part of the public sector income in all countries, thereby indicating what the most important types of taxes and duties to finance public sector activities are. This is not to neglect the other types as they can be important as part of the total public sector revenue.

All types of taxes and duties have different arguments in favour and against. This is shown in Table 6.1. Table 6.1 includes not only taxes and duties, but also user charges as this is a way of financing public sector spending, even though it is not a tax (see the definition in Chapter 5). The table also indicates where in Europe the instrument is mainly used, and this can also be seen by the data in Figure 6.1. This is a clear indication that when implementing changes in the tax structure, one needs to have a clear knowledge and awareness so that one can choose the best combination based upon national preferences. The table also indicates that there does not have to be a big difference between all types of public sector funding. Income tax and social security contributions can have the same overall economic consequences even though there may be consequences for who gets access to social benefits, for example.

User charges can be found in most countries, especially in relation to a number of services such as transport (trains, buses, road taxes), day-care

Table 6.1   Pros and cons of different ways of financing public sector spending

Main tax instruments	Advantages	Disadvantages	Used in
Income tax	Can ensure a high level of revenue and can be made progressive. Can be made both on wage earners and companies	Risk of changing balance between work and leisure, especially with high marginal tax rates	All European countries, especially Nordic countries
Value Added Tax	Relatively simple, and can vary between types of goods, for example, low or zero on foods. Will also be paid by tourists and those not paying income tax	Might have a negative impact on distribution as persons with lower income tend to have a higher propensity to consume	All European countries, especially Southern and Eastern countries
Duties	Can be targeted to luxury goods and might thereby have a positive impact on distribution. Can also help to enhance a better environment	Administration, and, if not targeted an upside-down effect	To a varying degree in all European countries, however Southern and Eastern to a higher degree
Social security contributions	Simple and effective, and ensure financing of welfare activities	Risk that those outside the labour market are not covered	Especially in the central continental and liberal welfare model countries in Europe
User charges	Increase the information on consumers' preferences and are paid by those receiving the services	Risk that those with low income do not get the service or not at the right time	Especially used in the healthcare area, but also transport, day-care for children in many EU countries
Others	Can be a way to tax inheritance, wealth, housing	Mainly administrative, but also possible negative side-effects in relation to mobility	Only more limited, and with a very varied structure

Source: Greve (2020).

for children, healthcare and long-term care. The main reasons for using user charges are:

(a) To raise revenue
(b) To regulate demand
(c) To improve allocative efficiency
(d) To prevent abuse.

User charges can thereby be seen as an attempt to apply market mechanisms in order to improve efficiency in the supply of public services. The theoretical argument is that people's demands are higher when they do not have to pay for a good and thus by free provision the correct preference revelation does not take place (see more in Chapter 8).

A common trend in taxation (to be returned to in Chapter 10) has been a lowering of corporate tax as part of international cooperation to attract companies and jobs in different countries.

One discussion is whether taxes and duties can affect economic growth and how they might do so. This applies to more or less economic growth. Special taxation of companies is argued to reduce economic growth because it should reduce companies' desire to invest. High marginal taxes on labour are also seen by some as having an effect on economic growth if they lead to a shortage of labour. Although it cannot be ruled out that very high taxes can affect economic growth, there is hardly any evidence for this, which is also due to the fact that there is still an economic incentive to make money (Cournède, Fournier, and Hoeller 2018; Hagemann 2018). In addition, the level of taxation cannot be seen independently of what the taxes are used for (cf. also Chapter 11 on a social investment perspective).

Overall, albeit with differences across countries, there seems to be a positive impact of increases in public sector spending through the multiplier effect, again also dependent on the actual economic situation in each country (Collingro and Frenkel 2020; Deleidi, Iafrate, and Levrero 2020).

These types of impact have to be seen also in the light of the possible impact on the economic distribution (see Chapter 5).

There has also been a debate on whether one can finance public sector expenditure with a deficit in the longer run. One argument is that the rational agents will foresee that there will then be an increase in taxation later, thus reducing the option for an effective expansionary fiscal policy, and the opposite with a surplus, where a reduction in spending will not reduce demand (King 2015). The issue of public sector deficit is returned to in Chapter 10.

6.5   CONCLUSIONS

It is really only the imagination that sets the limits for what types of taxes and duties can be used (cf. also the historical examples in Chapter 5). This does not change the fact that it is important to know how and in what way taxes and duties affect many different factors in a society and that there can be both advantages and disadvantages to different choices.

In addition, they can have different multiplier effects, and thus also the classical discussion of a possible balancing of efficiency with equality (Okun 1975). Therefore, decisions need to keep an eye on how different instruments work, including in combination with each other. What economic situation a country is in is also important, for example, in periods of recession there is a need for expansive instruments, but conversely in periods of boom so that the public sector can contribute to a more balanced economic development, which at the same time creates greater security for the individual citizen.

NOTE

1.   Here data from the OECD are used. The OECD and Eurostat are, in general, very good databases for comparative analysis as data are compiled in a systematic way for all countries. This not to neglect the fact that, especially when it comes to taxation, there can be hidden elements and not always compliance with regard to paying taxes and duties.

REFERENCES

Collingro, Franziska, and Michael Frenkel. 2020. "Fiscal Multipliers in the Euro Area: A Comparative Study." *The Quarterly Review of Economics and Finance*. https://doi .org/10.1016/j.qref.2020.08.005.

Constâncio, Vítor. 2020. "The Return of Fiscal Policy and the Euro Area Fiscal Rule." *Comparative Economic Studies* 62 (3): 358–72.

Cournède, Boris, Jean-Marc Fournier, and Peter Hoeller. 2018. "Public Finance Structure and Inclusive Growth," no. 25. https://doi.org/10.1787/e99683b5-en.

Deleidi, Matteo, Francesca Iafrate, and Enrico Sergio Levrero. 2020. "Public Investment Fiscal Multipliers: An Empirical Assessment for European Countries." *Structural Change and Economic Dynamics* 52: 354–65.

Greve, B. 2020. *Welfare and the Welfare State: Central Issues Now and in the Future*. Oxon: Routledge.

Hagemann, Robert. 2018. "Tax Policies for Inclusive Growth," no. 24. https://doi.org/ 10.1787/09ba747a-en.

King, John Edward. 2015. *Advanced Introduction to Post Keynesian Economics*. Cheltenham, UK and Northampton, MA, USA: Edward Elgar Publishing.

OECD. 2021. *Government at a Glance 2021*. https://doi.org/10.1787/1c258f55-en.

Okun, Arthur M. 1975. *Equality and Efficiency: The Big Tradeoff*. Washington, DC: Brookings Institution Press.

7. Steering of the public sector economy

7.1 INTRODUCTION

Even when a decision has been made about what the public sector should deliver, there is a need for knowledge about how the public sector's economy can be managed in the best possible way so that maximum benefit from the public sector activities is achieved, that is, efficient use of the scarce resources.

This requires first of all knowledge of management methods and management paths, as well as expertise of how to get the best possible data and make decisions based upon existing evidence. Emphasis is placed on being able to explain possible reasons for inefficient production, as well as methods for obtaining the best possible knowledge as a background for decisions and possible ways to influence citizens' behaviour, for example, through nudging.

Looking into management and steering is the first topic (Section 7.2) to deal with. This includes the theoretical understanding of the principal–agent relationship. The reason is that even if one knows what the best method to be used is in order to get the best results, then there is the need to know how to implement it.

The public sector will be understood not only as the individual organization or branch, but also as being across sectors and decision makers, for example, where there are both central and decentralized elements in the public sector delivery and regulation of societal development.

Section 7.3 focuses on what knowledge is needed in order to make the most effective choices. The principles are presented, however, without a highly detailed review of the many and very diverse methodological issues this raises. This is central as decisions made without the use of the best available knowledge can lead to ineffective use of the resources.

Section 7.4 looks briefly at how behavioural economics not only can be used internally in the public sector, but also at how it can be a way of influencing citizens' behaviour. Section 7.5 concludes the chapter.

7.2 INTERNAL STEERING OF THE PUBLIC SECTOR

The following looks at regulation internally in the public sector, and thus not, for example, legal regulation of citizens' and companies' behaviour. This is despite the fact that (as also stated in Chapter 3) regulation of market failures can take place through, for example, requirements for companies or citizens in what they may and may not do. Instead, the focus here is on how it is possible by other means to regulate behaviour in the public sector and thus ensure that the scarce resources are used as optimally as possible.

The principal–agent theory is central to understand one of the issues related to optimizing the use of resources. The theory describes that the principal has a task to be performed well and knows what it wants to be delivered (this could be more or better care for children or the elderly, for example). The principal does not necessarily know whether the agent can and/or will perform the task in the most efficient way. This is because there is information asymmetry, including that the agents who are to perform the tasks may have some professional perceptions of the best way to perform a task. Thus both intrinsic as well as extrinsic motivation factors may be at play, implying that what the principal wants to be delivered might not, for a possible number of reasons, be provided.

In public (as well as in private) organizations, there are in fact many and very different principals as well as agents. The tasks of the public sector are solved both centrally and decentrally in most countries, and there are also tasks where the public sector has agreed that private companies must perform the tasks in question. This entails a need to be able to know how tasks are best performed and what requirements can be made of the employees in an organization – regardless of whether one is looking at administration, childcare, teaching or transport. So, no matter what task, there will be a need for knowledge about whether the duties are performed in as best and cheapest a way as possible. A principal can also be an agent in another relationship. For example, a large hospital may have a director who is the principal in relation to the hospital, but at the same time is the agent in relation to those who finance the activity (typically the state). In any hierarchical system there will be a number of agents and principals. Thus, one might also need to analyse and understand who is principal and who is agent, and how the different levels interact.

Even when you know who the agent is and who the principal is, there will be a need to find the best way to achieve the results that the principal wants to achieve.

It is not theoretically possible to argue for what will always be the best way of doing things, but instead there will be a need to assess on a case-to-case basis which form will be the best. This can range from, for example, setting the requirements for the number of treatments, to providing financial incentives to achieve certain goals, including, for example, a high degree of user satisfaction or maintenance of a building, cleaning of various areas or better quality of education. Which requirements to ask from the agent require an often more detailed analysis of the different areas, including possible variations in different countries.

It is often desired that there should be as few transaction costs as possible for both public and private activities. Therefore, setting simple and clear goals may be desirable, but at the same time the principal–agent theory illustrates that there will be a need for control measures in the public sector's activities. This applies in relation not only to the employees' efforts, but also to complying with existing legislation, regardless of whether it is about the speed of traffic, requirements for the working environment or that the taxes and duties that are required are paid.

There is also a need to decide which investments should be initiated and which should not. For this, cost-benefit and cost-effectiveness analysis can be used (see more in Section 7.4).

Thus, deciding how to manage and steer the public sector to ensure the goals of the public sector activities are reached, as well as being done in the best way, is not an easy task. This also helps in explaining why there is a need to know what the best intervention is. This is the focus of the next section.

7.3   EVIDENCE-BASED STEERING

Knowledge is not a constant. New knowledge and new analyses that contribute to knowing better how different types of interventions have an effect are constantly emerging. The public sector will, again, to get the most out of scarce resources, also need to use this knowledge. It helps to understand why there has been an increasing focus on having evidence-based knowledge about which efforts work best, but also understandings that it is not so simple in all areas to ensure that there is solid knowledge, and that this can change over time, just as knowledge can be neglected by both companies and policy makers. For a number of details and discussions related to both collecting and using evidence, including the risk of doing so, see a number of articles in Greve (2017), including also more details of a number of methodological challenges when conducting the different types of analysis. A definition of economic evaluation that can be useful to have in mind is: "the systematic attempt to identify, measure and compare the costs and outcomes of alternative interventions" (Sefton et al. 2002, 5). It could as well be important to "consider what would have happened in the absence of the intervention being evaluated" (Sefton et al. 2002, 7)

All knowledge is not of equal quality, and all knowledge can change and when new research provides new insights this needs to be considered for use although there is still a need to also analyse the cost of implementing this. There is therefore talk of a hierarchy of evidence (Figure 7.1).

Figure 7.1 shows that systematic evidence is the best, given this evidence systematizes a number of studies, and the best of which are a number of randomized controlled trials. Slight variations in how this hierarchy looks and what

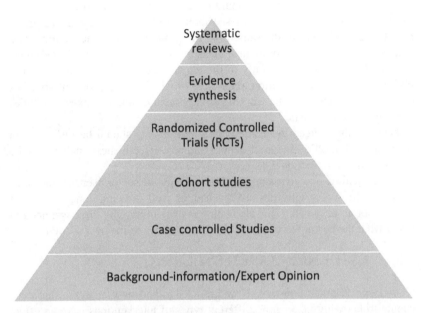

Figure 7.1   Evidence hierarchy

to include can be found (see e.g. Sundberg 2017). However, overall, there is agreement on the structure of the best types of knowledge to use.

This does not mean that in all areas it is equally simple to find systematic knowledge or to be able to collect randomized data, for example, in areas where social interactions are important, such as large parts of the social area. But this does not change the need to be able to gather the best possible knowledge in order to provide citizens with the best service for the least possible expenses.

Applying the best possible knowledge does not mean that no better knowledge can come later or that no attempt should be made to find better solutions, but rather to recognize that all ways of organizing and solving problems are not the best. This knowledge could come into conflict with professionals' perception that they know best in the individual situation as to what is the best effort, because whether this is actually the case can be difficult to determine. In all cases, the professional cannot be updated with the latest knowledge and thus risks providing a poorer service than is possible. Conversely, it makes sense to include knowledge from people who perform different services in order to increase the knowledge of what works best.

For example, for many years there has been a tradition in the field of health to set the requirements in order to document that new medicine works and without major side-effects. Even if it works better, there is still the need to set this in relation to the price for the new product. Thus, even if we know what is the best, for example, medicine, one needs to compare the efficiency of the intervention with the perhaps also higher cost of the intervention. If, for example, a new, much more expensive intervention improves the situation to a very limited extent, this might be an argument for continuing with the existing treatment. This overall implies a trade-off between cost and impact, and within health economics there are, as an example, a number of ways to compare different interventions. This might involve normative issues on the value of life and life-quality. Again, also that if spending more money on a new intervention with only a limited improvement, this might be at the risk of having to reduce spending in other areas.

A risk of using a single case study may also be that it has been conducted in special circumstances (perhaps the resources available, special cases or with greater commitment, better management or a combination thereof). At the same time, it is not a given fact that such special circumstances can be transferred to other places, and thus that expected effects will be absent. Still, again having a case study indicating new approaches can be the first attempt to find new ways, so this is not to argue that one should not use case studies, but more to be aware that they can not necessarily be used to generalize the situation of what is best in other circumstances.

Overall, the collection and assessment of methods and efforts within a large number of the public sector's economy has been important to ensure the best possible use of the scarce resources, and that citizens receive the best possible treatment within the given economic resources available. This also implies that there is still a need to try out new ways of solving societal problems, and that new knowledge is constantly emerging that can be used, again for the sake of both citizens and the public sector economy, and for more efficient services to be provided within one area, which will then provide an opportunity to use more resources within another area or reduce taxes and fees.

7.4   COST-BENEFIT AND COST-EFFECTIVENESS STUDIES

Cost-benefit analysis is one way to find out which investment will be the most effective to do. This is done by assessing the cost of investments and the economic benefits that come out of an investment based on the best possible data and valued in the same unit, commonly a monetary value. This also done using the alternative cost approach, that is, money spent on one task can't be used on another task, and these analyses might help in making the best informed decision.

As the benefits typically come after the investment, it is important that these are discounted to the time the investment is made in order to be able to compare at the same price level. The problem here is that the interest rate (discount factor) used influences whether the investment proves to be sensible. The higher the factor, the less advantageous an investment will look. It therefore also means a great deal of uncertainty, especially for investments that are expected to have a long life, such as bridges, roads, and so on. At the same time, it can be difficult to determine the costs, as if there is high unemployment and those who are to carry out the project are unemployed, the wage cost must be set to zero, but if it is people who are already working then it must be priced based on the wages of the persons concerned. The usefulness of the investment can also be difficult to estimate, as it can be difficult to assess, for example, how many people will use a bridge, road, and so on. When it comes to the use of a new road, there is also the problem that there can be negative environmental effects if the establishment of a road entails greater private traffic and less use of public transport. This while if it reduces transport time at the same time is an improvement in the use of spare resources.

In addition, the benefit must be calculated in money, which will typically be done by assessing, in the case of a bridge, the time saved by using the new infrastructure multiplied by a price per hour such as average wage. Calculations should also include possible externalities arising from the investment, whether positive or negative. Once the calculation has been made, one can in principle argue economically for the investment if there is a positive value, and when choosing between several possible investments, use the one where the gain is greatest. There might be an issue that comparing across different policy fields can be difficult and therefore the approach is often mainly used when comparing initiatives within one field.

Evaluations of efforts also involve an assessment of how effective they are, but not necessarily an assessment of how the interplay between costs and benefits of an activity is.

Cost-effectiveness looks at which intervention, where one can expect roughly the same effect, is the cheapest to invest in. This presupposes that there is analysis of whether there are comparable efforts in relation to a specific problem (regardless of whether it is pollution, health, working environment, childcare, etc.). By then comparing the costs of an effort, the effort that is the most cost-effective can be chosen. For example, this can be which intervention has the best outcome of getting people back to the labour market, such as getting the most people back at the lowest cost per extra person in employment.

Efforts do not always have the same effect, for example, on the quality of life, and therefore there may also be a need to be able to compare initiatives where not only expenses, but also benefits can be recognized.

This requires several things to be able to make a calculation of what the best investment is:

(1)   That the benefits of an effort (e.g. better quality of life) can also be converted into a monetary value
(2)   That there is knowledge about how long the effort works
(3)   To decide which discount factor to choose.

There is no unequivocal agreement or knowledge on how to convert benefits into a monetary value in all areas, which is especially the case (cf. more in Chapter 9) when a better state of health or care for the elderly is to be valued. On the other hand, when assessing traffic projects, one, for example, can include, as mentioned above, saved transport time as a value by converting it with the average hourly wage in the labour market. Of course, it requires knowledge of how much of a time saving there is, and of how long it can be expected to last. At the same time, it may be necessary to include the environmental consequences of increased traffic. Valuation hereof might also be difficult.

Point 2 is important, as the expenditures of an investment today are calculated in today's prices, while the gains, if they come, will do so over a long period of time and must then be recalculated to today's prices in order for cost and benefits to be compared. This is because income in the future does not have the same value as does inflation. If it is possible for both expenses and income to use fixed prices, which normally, however, will not be possible, then this is less of an issue.

This makes point 3 important, as a higher discount factor will make long-term projects less profitable than a lower discount factor. So, the determination of the discount rate can have an impact on which, especially very long-term, investments, such as in infrastructure, housing and improvement of the environment, are sensible from a societal economic perspective and which are not. The long-term real interest rate on the capital market can be an indicator of which discount factor is to be used.

There will also be a need, as a minimum, for a discussion of uncertainties associated with an assessment of long-term investments, including assumptions of both cost and income from the investment. For example, in relation to a bridge, how many will use the bridge and the expected time savings, as well as how the increase in pollution from more traffic will be. This should be done in a transparent way as this is important in order for others also to judge the outcome of an investment. Uncertainties around the estimates of cost and benefits should also be described as best as possible.

In addition, once the investment has been completed, it is an irreversible process in the sense that the money has been spent and cannot be spent on any other projects. This is what is referred to as sunk-cost. It also means that if the price, to use for example a bridge, is to be as in a perfect competitive market, then it will have to be close to zero, as the price must reflect the marginal cost of keeping the bridge for the marginal extra person choosing to cross the bridge.

As mentioned, it will often be difficult to set a price on the benefits, and therefore analyses are more often used where comparisons of benefits (such as the number of services, their quality if measurable and the derived reduction in costs in other areas) are used between different initiatives.

Overall, there will be a need for a clear description of how the calculations are made, and given the uncertainty that will always be there, it is also necessary to provide an assessment of the project for different types of uncertainty calculations.

7.5   BEHAVIOURAL ECONOMICS

There is hardly anyone who constantly uses a rational utility-maximizing behaviour as an assumption in order to understand how citizens behave. This does not mean that no one behaves rationally and considers how they get the most satisfaction and enjoyment from their available resources and decisions, including the use of their money (as a scarce resource). Nor does it mean that there is not, on average, a high degree of change in behaviour, which means, for example, that the consumption of a product is affected if the price increases as a result of, for example, new taxes. But at the same time, in recent years there has been a focus on the fact that when citizens for various reasons do not have a sensible behaviour – often also in the long run – then there may be reasons to consider whether they can be "nudged" in a better direction. This is often labelled behavioural economics (for overview and presentation of central ideas see Wilkinson and Klaes 2017; Corr and Plagnol 2019).

A first historical example was that in Schiphol airport (Amsterdam) a picture of a fly was put in the urinals for men and this increased cleanliness as men, seemingly, were then better able to hit the urinal and reduce spillage on the floor by 80 per cent (Thaler and Sunstein 2008). Another example is that many people postpone saving for a pension to a later stage in their life, which might imply that the saving will be too small. Here, a nudge trying to make people start saving earlier would be helpful. It might also be possible to use behavioural insights to reduce the level of tax evasion (Pickhardt and Prinz 2014).

Living a healthy life can also be difficult. However, besides informing on the good life, small changes such as the availability of healthy foods in shops and canteens can help, as can making it easier to be active. There has also been a shortage of donors of heart, kidneys, and so on in many countries, and here, by reversing the decision-making structure, one can influence how many are willing to donate, so that the individual must make an active decision not to be a donor, rather than needing to decide to become a donor, and then persuading more people to become donors. This is because in a number of contexts, overall, 80 per cent will say yes to the automatic choice, whereas only 20 per cent will change. Nudging is described as libertarian paternalism influence, although with the individual being able to make another choice, but it will require a more conscious effort from the individual. Naturally, there is also an ethical discussion on how and to what extent one can and should use nudges as they might manipulate the individual. Still, as a way of changing behaviour in one direction, it can also be seen from a societal perspective that a better direction can improve the economic options for the public sector, also bearing in mind that it is possible to behave otherwise. To avoid confusion, it is important to be aware that nudging is an attempt to push people at least from a societal point of view in a better direction. Thus, a new tax or duty to change behaviour is not a nudge as the individual is not able to continue as usual and only able to avoid paying a new tax or duty by not buying the good.

Nudge can also be used, for example, to make it easier for citizens to find their way around a hospital by painting coloured lines that patients must follow instead of having to find out for themselves from the name of a ward. During COVID-19, arrows/lines have been drawn on floors in many countries, stating what the distance should be between customers and/or users and in which direction to walk in order to avoid crowds.

Thus, it is possible to use nudging and behavioural activities in order to change the behaviour of societies and individuals. In a number of ways and in different parts of societies, this has been used in many countries in recent years. Information on a number of ways of trying to use this approach can be found at https://www.oecd.org/gov/regulatory-policy/behavioural-insights .htm (accessed 6 August 2021).

There are a number of ways of influencing behaviour, as touched upon in several chapters, ranging from economic incentives, to legal requirements for companies in relation to monopoly and pollution, to criteria and demand to receivers of welfare benefits. The main aim here is to indicate that nudging is seen as another way to influence behaviour than more classical public sector economic approaches.

7.6   CONCLUSIONS

Although public sector economics is often about the impact of expenditure as well as taxes and duties, an important element of the public sector's activity is also to use public expenditure most efficiently. Therefore, internal governance in the public sector is also an element of the public sector economy. There are thus, as well as in the private sector, management tasks, and a need to get the best possible results. This involves trying to ensure that the best possible current knowledge is applied, and that efforts are based on evidence of what works, if available – both for the sake of the citizens and the public sector economy.

The chapter has also indicated that it is not only traditional financial management instruments that are available. It is also possible to try to nudge people to make better choices or, for example, live healthier lives. This is the explanation as to why behavioural economics is used to influence behaviour in a number of countries, and thus can be a relatively inexpensive instrument to use to ensure socially beneficial effects.

REFERENCES

Corr, P., and A. Plagnol. 2019. *Behavioral Economics – the Basics*. Oxon: Routledge.

Greve, B. 2017. *Handbook of Social Policy Evaluation*. 1st edn. Cheltenham, UK and Northampton, MA, USA: Edward Elgar Publishing. https://doi.org/10.4337/9781785363245.

Pickhardt, Michael, and Aloys Prinz. 2014. "Behavioral Dynamics of Tax Evasion – a Survey." *Journal of Economic Psychology*. https://doi.org/10.1016/j.joep.2013.08.006.

Sefton, Tom, Sarah Byford, David McDaid, John Hills, and Martin Knapp. 2002. "Making the Most of It." *Economic Evaluation in the Social Welfare Field*. York: Joseph Rowntree Foundation.

Sundberg, Trude. 2017. "Systematic Reviews in Social Policy Evaluation." In *Handbook of Social Policy Evaluation*, edited by B. Greve, 1st edn, 19. Cheltenham, UK and Northampton, MA, USA: Edward Elgar Publishing.

Thaler, Richard H., and Cass R. Sunstein. 2008. *Nudge: Improving Decisions about Health, Wealth, and Happiness*. London: Yale University Press.

Wilkinson, Nick, and Matthias Klaes. 2017. *An Introduction to Behavioral Economics*. London: Macmillan International Higher Education.

8. In-cash benefits – the role of the public sector

8.1 INTRODUCTION

Using the theoretical arguments of public sector intervention as presented earlier in the book, this chapter looks specifically into core in-cash benefits in different welfare state areas. These elements of public sector activity are presented as they are of great importance for the living standard of large groups in societies, and in most developed economies they make up a very large part of the total public sector expenditure.

The chapter is organized so that the different benefits are used as key cases to inform and discuss the above-mentioned issues, albeit social investment is looked at in more detail in Chapter 11.

Thus in Section 8.2 social policy is the central issue, including why there can be efficiency gains to achieve if benefits are provided collectively instead of by individual payments and/or insurance. The section also includes part of the discussion of the variations and possible consequences of user charges. Pensions are given a specific section (8.3) due to its nature as a very central in-cash benefit.

Passive labour market policy also includes important benefits, and the possible logics underpinning them is the aim of Section 8.4, in relation to central benefits such as social assistance and unemployment, as well as early retirement benefits. Given the possible link to incentives, a short depiction of other benefits and the principles behind them is also included. Section 8.5 then sums up the chapter.

8.2 SOCIAL POLICY

Social policy has a role in many types and varieties of intervention. It also uses a variety of instruments to achieve the set goals. For example, ensuring a minimum income on the labour market can be reached in different ways, as well as having some arguments in favour and some against. A conservative liberal might argue for a low level, a living wage liberal for a higher level and adjusting for living costs, whereas in social democratic states high wage floors might be done by collective bargaining (Wilson 2021).

Social protection systems can have a variety of roles, where it has been argued that there can be a split between a preventive function, a protective function and a promotive function (Loewe and Schüring 2021). This includes the relation to the level of poverty and the ability to prevent further damage for a person/family, including the size of the social policy income transfers. Risk to be covered can be related to life-cycle risks (from cradle to grave), health risks and job loss/unemployment.

We know that countries with high public spending on social policy generally have a higher level of subjective well-being (Kolev and Tassot 2016), and we have also seen that the richer welfare states in the Northern part of Europe are all often at the top of the world happiness lists (Martela et al. 2020). Thus, there is an impact on overall societal development by the spending and activities within social policy. This does not reduce the need for ways in which to prioritize and decide on the level and approach of delivering social policy.

Social policy is a very broad area, and here the focus is mainly on principles in relation to in-cash benefits.

Disregarding hospital services, cash benefits have been the first to be systematically developed in modern societies, starting with Bismarck's reforms in Germany in the 1880s, and often also labelled old social risk. The logic was that they should to a large extent provide citizens with compensation for loss of income in connection with social risks, such as old age, illness, accidents at work and unemployment. Having a principle of compensation for loss of income in connection with a social risk (historically: pension, sickness, unemployment and work injury) originally said, as it does today, nothing about what the level that should be. There are several explanations for this, which point in different directions:

(1) there is limited overall financial scope
(2) money spent on an in-cash benefit will then not be able to be used in another area (the alternative cost)
(3) the way in which benefits affect incentives, including, particularly, in relation to work
(4) the benefit can be used as a contribution to automatic stabilizers, understood in the sense that if, for example, unemployment grows, citizens still have the means (income) to buy goods and services.

This shows that social policy is not only about the welfare of the individual citizen, but also about how expenditure can have an impact on the overall economy and its activities. The above reflect the issues with regard not only to the aforementioned old social risk, but also new social risk, such as divorce, lone-parents and the work–family balance.

One issue to understand is that the central aspect of social policy is the combined marginal tax and benefit rate. This reflects the percentage to be paid in tax, reduction/increase in social benefits or paying more/less in user fees when the income changes. This can mean that there is very little left, and it could affect the incentive to take a job or work more. At the same time, however, the magnitude of the impact depends on whether the payment, for example, for childcare, can reduce income tax payments, which is possible in many European countries.[1] Thus, it is also the net payments that should be used when calculating the combined rate in combination with the marginal income tax rate. Thereby also discussing economic incentives to work or not to work is a question not only of the marginal tax rate, but also the influence of user charges, as well as possible reductions in other social benefits. This is because, for example, housing benefits in most countries are dependent on the income of the household.

This shows that user charges can have different implications (using day-care for children as an example), so that they can:

(1)   Influence the marginal combined tax and benefit ratio
(2)   Indicate willingness to pay
(3)   Influence equality in access to day-care
(4)   Influence labour supply.

This will then have to be combined with a discussion on the possible benefits for children, as well as an awareness that looking only at one element in economic decisions can imply that not all types of impact are included.

The impact will depend on the type of user charges, where one at least can have the following types:

(1)   A percentage of the cost of producing the service
(2)   A percentage, as in 1, but with a ceiling on the payment
(3)   A percentage, as in 1 or 2, but depending on the income of the person/ household
(4)   A fixed amount, possibly depending on age or, for example, disability.

These four types will have different effects on both incentives and the distribution, which at the same time are influenced by what percentage is paid by the users and what percentage by the state, but also depends on how large the expenses are. The percentage can also have an effect on the extent to which the payment can be understood as revealing the users' preferences, as the lower the percentage, the less it tells about preferences, and can further obscure people's knowledge of the actual costs of producing a service. At the same time, there is

Table 8.1   *Possible criteria for access to in-cash benefits*

	In-cash benefit
Age	Pension, child benefit
Unemployed	Unemployment benefit or social assistance
Need	Social assistance
Sick	Sickness benefit
Low income	Social assistance, housing benefit
Non-work ability/people with disabilities	Early retirement/disability pension

Source: Own depiction.

a risk (cf. more in Chapter 9 on health) that a high user fee deters some people from using different services, including paying for the necessary medicine.

A user payment independent of income, and possibly wealth, will have a regressive effect because everyone must pay the same, meaning that it will be relatively more expensive for low-income groups than for others.

Overall, the implication is that one carefully needs to consider the consequences of user charges, even though, naturally, they can also be a way to finance public sector spending and ensure that users will reveal their preferences by paying the user charge.

Social in-cash benefits can be awarded according to a wide range of very different criteria, examples of which are given in Table 8.1.

There may be different logics and rationales behind the choices of criteria, for example that cash benefits go mainly to people with limited or no income and/or wealth. This may be out of a desire to limit public spending or ensure a more equal distribution of consumption opportunities in a society. This also includes the fact that certain benefits to people with disabilities are given as a way to compensate for the extra cost of living compared to people without disabilities. They are, therefore, also often not related to the income and/or wealth of the persons.

There are very different criteria in different countries, including a ceiling on the amount to be received for a large number of social benefits.

An example of one criterion is child benefit for children under a certain age, the level of which can then vary according to age, just as it can be in-cash or as a reduction in the tax to be paid. It might or might not be means-tested, that is, dependent on the income and/or wealth in a household.

Age is typically also a criterion for receiving public old-age pension benefits (see more in Section 8.3), and therefore the age at which a person can receive an old-age pension is not the same in all countries. A disability pension relates to whether a person is able to support him/herself and is based on medical tests indicating that the person will not be able to work at all or only to a very limited extent.

Housing benefits in most countries depend on the cost of renting one's home and the person's income, and possibly also wealth. The logic is that the services must be targeted at the people who have the greatest need to receive these services. The degree of targeting of social benefits can be determined not only on the basis of economic logics, but will also be embedded in more normative considerations of who needs these and at what level.

There are further benefits related to maternal and paternal leave, sickness and industrial injury, where in all cases the ability to receive the benefits depends on whether the social situation exists. Unemployment benefit is discussed later in the chapter.

The size of the benefit often has a relation to the ability to finance public sector expenditure, but also the possible impact on incentives to work, as well as the degree of legitimacy among voters for various types of benefits. There might further be means-testing (income and/or wealth) so that in order to receive benefits it is not sufficient just to fulfil the criteria of age, but also the person's economic situation must be taken into account. Means-testing can be for the individual, but can also be for the household, which is, as an example, typically for housing benefits. There is, theoretically, no clear knowledge of what a too high level of benefit is, because people are influenced by not only economic incentives, but also aspects such as social contacts and having something to do (Brooks 2011).

In addition to the previously stated arguments and principles related to benefits, for example, on the impact of incentives, there might also be other issues at stake. One example is the ability to redistribute between families with children and families without children.

Thus, as one of the three core issues as presented in Chapter 2, the public sector affects the distribution, and not only between "rich" and "poor", but also between different groups in society. Whether higher child family benefits can affect fertility is not documented, but it contributes to children growing up in poverty to a lesser extent (depending on the size of the benefit), and thus (cf. Chapter 10) can also be an expression of a social investment mindset. Family benefits can thus have a different rationale than other benefits, and whether they are means-tested or not varies across countries.

Social policy can thus have a vertical as well as a horizontal impact on the distribution, where the horizontal is between different socio-economic groups (e.g. with and without children). The vertical is sometimes also referred to as the Robin Hood effect, that is, from rich to poor. Economic analysis, as mentioned in previous chapters, cannot say anything about how large these benefits should be, but can inform policy makers, especially with the aid of empirical examinations, as to what the consequences may be.

Table 8.2   *In-cash and in-kind benefits as percentages of GDP in 2019*
                 in European countries

	In-kind benefits	In-cash benefits	Total	In-cash as percentages of total
EU28	9.4	17.1	26.5	64.5%
Belgium	9.1	18.4	27.5	66.9%
Bulgaria	5.4	10.6	16.1	65.8%
Czechia	6.4	12.0	18.4	65.2%
Denmark	12.9	17.1	30.0	57.0%
Germany	11.4	17.7	29.1	60.8%
Estonia	5.0	11.1	16.1	68.9%
Ireland	5.4	7.6	13.0	58.5%
Greece	4.9	19.8	24.8	79.8%
Spain	7.3	16.4	23.7	69.2%
France	11.4	20.0	31.4	63.7%
Croatia	7.7	13.7	21.4	64.0%
Italy	6.6	21.7	28.3	76.7%
Cyprus	5.0	13.3	18.3	72.7%
Latvia	4.7	10.7	15.5	69.0%
Lithuania	5.4	10.8	16.1	67.1%
Luxembourg	6.6	14.7	21.3	69.0%
Hungary	5.7	10.6	16.3	65.0%
Malta	6.3	8.9	15.2	58.6%
Netherlands	10.3	16.7	27.0	61.9%
Austria	9.3	19.3	28.6	67.5%
Poland	5.3	15.6	21.0	74.3%
Portugal	6.7	16.5	23.2	71.1%
Romania	4.9	10.1	15.0	67.3%
Slovenia	7.6	14.2	21.8	65.1%
Slovakia	6.1	11.4	17.4	65.5%
Finland	11.8	17.7	29.5	60.0%
Sweden	12.9	14.3	27.2	52.6%
UK	10.1	15	25.5	60.4%

Note: For EU-28 and the UK the data are from 2018.
Source: Eurostat, SPR_EXP_FTO, accessed 6 January 2022.

In Europe there is a difference in the spending on in-cash and in-kind benefits, as depicted in Table 8.2.

In all countries, in-cash benefit is the largest proportion of social spending, but it varies from around half to around ¾. Historical preferences, including variations in the development of a number of services, such as day-care for children, also help in explaining the variation. Criteria, level of benefit and areas also vary. For example, in a large number of countries, pensions is the most important area. The level of spending on unemployment benefit varies further due to generosity, but also due to the impact of the business cycle.

8.3 PENSIONS

Pensions was, as mentioned earlier, one of the first social risks to be covered in many countries. As a consequence of more people moving to cities and having no other income when they got older and could no longer work, state pensions were established. These were typically social insurance schemes, but also government schemes where, after a means-test, people who had reached a certain age could have access to a, relative to today, very modest pension benefit.

Most countries today have universal public pension systems, but they vary considerably, including the interplay between public and private pension schemes, which is discussed later in this section.

There are two fundamentally different ways of financing pensions. One is a pay-as-you-go (PAYG) system and the other is a fund-based scheme. They can, in principle, be combined so that some part of the pension is based on savings in a pension fund and some that is from a PAYG system.

There are pros and cons to both approaches.

The pros of a PAYG system are that it is simple to change the level of the benefits; it might eliminate the risk of inflation for pensioners; and it gives a possible higher return on investments (assuming that money not saved by individual for the future when retiring is spent on investment), which is higher than interest rates. The cons are that it does not necessarily raise resources for paying pensions; it might have a negative impact on saving; if it increases tax rates, it can have a negative influence on work incentives and a risk of a lower level of competitiveness.

For the fund-based scheme, the pros are that it can increase capital stock; it does not look like a tax and thereby has fewer distortions; and the government more precisely knows the level of public expenditure in the future. The cons are that it will take a long time to implement changes in the level of the benefits; it is problematic to ensure the effective investment of funds; there is a risk of a too high level of saving; and if the government can then reduce spending on public pensions, it can increase spending in other areas even more.

At the same time, pension systems can be universal, that is, based on citizenship and/or, typically, on legal residence in a country for a shorter or longer period. But they can also be combined in a number of different ways, which is why pension systems are often referred to as a pillar system. Typically, a three-pillar system.

They are:

(1)   Public pension system
(2)   Labour market based
(3)   Individual savings (Hinrichs 2019).

The public pension system may be characterized as Bismarckian or Beveridgian. In the former, pensions are based on social security contributions, and in the latter, they are financed out of general taxes and fees.

These two types do not have to imply a big difference in economic impact, whereas there can be a difference depending on whether the pension is a defined benefit, or whether it is only defined what is to be paid into the pension or how many years a person, for example, must have worked or stayed in a country to get a pension. The pension is then calculated based upon the contributions made, which then can imply inequality in living conditions for the elderly.

Labour market-based pensions are typically linked to employers paying a pension contribution into a pension fund, sometimes labelled occupational welfare (Farnsworth 2019). This can be agreed in a collective agreement or in an individual agreement with the company. It is thus a fund-based pension system, which in addition can be supported by the fact that it can reduce the payment of income tax, so-called fiscal welfare or also referred to as tax expenditures (Morel, Touzet, and Zemmour 2018; Sinfield 2019). There may also be a tax rebate on the individual savings.

In addition, there may be criteria for the age at which a pension can be paid out. In the EU, for example, one can also earn a pension called a fractional pension, which means that a person who has worked in several countries can receive a national pension from several countries based on the number of years worked in each of them (i.e. each country). Also, a minimum number of years can be set for collective or private pension saving. One reason for this is to avoid the risk of reducing the labour supply from early retirement by those who have amassed the necessary savings to maintain their living standard in retirement.

The size of the pension, like other social benefits, can also depend on any other income of persons (including personal or labour market pension) that may have an impact on the state pension. Similarly, wealth can theoretically have significance, dependent on the specific rules in each pension system.

There can thus be a large number of interactions in relation to the standard of living for old-age pensioners between the social benefits, personal savings and other income. Pensions vary considerably from country to country, as does, therefore, the risk of living in poverty (Ebbinghaus, Nelson, and Nieuwenhuis 2020).

Trends in recent years have been for a higher age of retirement, a stronger significance of contributions, changes in indexation of benefits, but also in some countries larger minimum benefits (Hinrichs 2021).

Despite these many issues, the public pension system still plays an important role for people who have left the labour market due to age, and is a central element to reduce poverty in old age.

In addition, a number of countries have disability-related pensions, which often depend on the ability to work, and thus, for example, can be given after a work accident. The level of benefit is dependent on the degree of disability, both of which vary across countries.

8.4 UNEMPLOYMENT AND OTHER SOCIAL BENEFITS

This section looks into the benefits related to what is called passive labour market policy, but also a number of other benefits financed by the public sector.

There are two types of what is termed passive labour market policies. One is unemployment benefit, the other is the possibility of early retirement benefit.

Here, the balance and discussions are related to how high financial compensation for the unemployed should be. The economic argument is that too high a level, without being able, theoretically, to define what level will imply a too strong decline in labour supply, and further then leads to too few incentives to take a vacant job in the labour market, and thus risks that some are unemployed for longer than necessary. Conversely, a higher level of unemployment benefits from an economic point of view could act as an automatic stabilizer in a country's economic development, as people who become unemployed can continue to pay their bills and buy food and goods, thus reducing the risk of greater fluctuations in a country's economic activity. There may also be a consideration for the distribution in society in order to prevent anyone from living in poverty.

Unemployment benefits can theoretically be established via a market-based, insurance-based unemployment benefit system. The problem with this may be that the risk of becoming unemployed differs across different occupational groups, and people with low risk will stay within the same insurance scheme and have a low payment, whereas people with high risk of unemployment will have to pay a higher insurance premium.

In addition, in a privately based system, higher transaction costs will be needed to determine in which group the individual is to be placed, that is, to ensure that there is a connection between the risk of unemployment and the insurance price, including as a result of asymmetric information, and thus the risk of adverse selection.

As in other fields, there can also be a risk of moral hazards with this type of insurance, that is, an insured person may be less worried about becoming unemployed and thus behaves in a way that increases the risk of this.

Conversely, most people of working age want a job, and the risk of becoming unemployed, as well as being unemployed, has a negative effect on individual well-being (Helliwell and Huang 2014; Hijzen and Menyhert 2016; Inanc 2018). It will therefore counteract the risk of a high degree of moral hazard in relation to unemployment insurance.

There will be people who are not able to work until they reach the retirement age given in a country, and therefore in a number of countries there are opportunities for early retirement. In relation to financial compensation, the balance here is between how generous it should be, with the risk of many retiring, and the economic living conditions of people who are physically or mentally incapacitated – will they be able to live a good life when they no longer work? How to set the level also depends on the ability to finance the public sector.

The focus above has especially been on unemployment benefit, and a number of the same arguments also apply to social assistance, which is the lowest safety-net in many countries. As with unemployment benefit, there can be requirements for those receiving the benefit (see more in Chapter 9 on active labour market policy). Whereas unemployment benefit is often connected to the individual, social assistance can include rules related to who should be responsible for other family members, depending on the family composition. Also, social assistance is often more restrictive only as to who has access and under which conditions.

There is a need to have a place to live. Therefore, in a number of countries it is possible to get support to pay for accommodation. The size of the support depends on the cost of renting a place, but typically also the household income, the number of children, as well as the size of the housing. Thus a large number of elements can be included in the calculation, the idea being to try to balance the need for support and the legitimacy of the benefit. For example, people receiving support might thereby be enabled to have a better standard of housing than those who have to pay for themselves, and also a high level of state support might increase rents because people would still be able to afford the higher rent. Thus, such kind of deadweight loss needs to be taken into consideration. Furthermore, housing support is typically only for rented homes and not owner-occupied housing. Thus, also these systems can be, and are, often very complicated.[2]

There are further benefits related to both maternity and paternity leave, and also in some countries support to take care of a frail person. One will have to investigate this individually in each country as there is a large variety of approaches to benefits, albeit they commonly relate to impact on incentives, fiscal costs and automatic stabilizers, as well as the legitimacy of the benefits.

8.5 SUMMING UP

This chapter has presented a number of cash benefits with a focus on the economic justifications and arguments for and against public sector involvement in the delivery of various types of benefits. They are also related to market failures as well as possible distributional effects of different choices. This includes discussions about incentives, especially income transfers such as those related to unemployment benefits.

Even if it is decided that the public sector must provide a number of services or income transfers, this does not give any indication of how generous they should be. This also includes in relation to the allocation of resources, the distribution of abilities in a society and the possible impact when they function as automatic stabilizers.

The provision of cash benefits will ultimately depend on the willingness to finance the public sector, and prioritization between different areas. This prioritization is ultimately a political decision, but may, based on economic analysis, be influenced by, for example, the possible impact on labour supply or saving. It is important to be aware of not only the possible direct costs, but also the longer-term impact on societies' development.

NOTES

1. See https://www.oecd.org/els/soc/benefits-and-wages/Net%20childcare%20cos ts%20in%20EU%20countries_2019.pdf, accessed 29 October, 2021, where information on the size of the combined rate can be found.
2. For details of country systems, see https://www.ssa.gov/policy/docs/progdesc/ ssptw/2018-2019/europe/index.html, and also comparative tables for Europe can be found at: https://www.missoc.org/missoc-database/comparative-tables/, accessed 8 December 2021.

REFERENCES

Brooks, David. 2011. *The Social Animal. The Hidden Sources of Love, Character, and Achievement.* New York: Random House.
Ebbinghaus, B., K. Nelson, and R. Nieuwenhuis. 2020. "Poverty in Old Age." In *The Routledge International Handbook of Poverty*, edited by B. Greve, 1st edn, 256–67. Oxon: Routledge.
Farnsworth, Kevin. 2019. "Occupational Welfare." In *The Routledge Handbook of the Welfare State*, edited by B. Greve, 2nd edn, 34–45. Oxon: Routledge.

Helliwell, John F., and Haifang Huang. 2014. "New Measures of the Costs of Unemployment: Evidence from the Subjective Well-being of 3.3 Million Americans." *Economic Inquiry* 52 (4): 1485–502.

Hijzen, Alexander, and Balint Menyhert. 2016. "Measuring Labour Market Security and Assessing Its Implications for Individual Well-being." Paris: OECD.

Hinrichs, Karl. 2019. "Old Age and Pensions." In *The Routledge Handbook of the Welfare State*, edited by B. Greve, 2nd ed., 418–31. Oxon: Routledge.

Hinrichs, Karl. 2021. "Recent Pension Reforms in Europe: More Challenges, New Directions. An Overview." *Social Policy & Administration* 55 (3): 409–22. https://doi.org/10.1111/spol.12712.

Inanc, Hande. 2018. "Unemployment, Temporary Work, and Subjective Well-being: The Gendered Effect of Spousal Labor Market Insecurity." *American Sociological Review* 83 (3): 536–66.

Kolev, Alexandre, and Caroline Tassot. 2016. "Can Investments in Social Protection Contribute to Subjective Well-being?" OECD, no. 332. https://doi.org/10.1787/5jlz3k7pqc5j-en.

Loewe, Markus, and Esther Schüring. 2021. "Introduction to the Handbook on Social Protection Systems." In *Handbook on Social Protection Systems*, edited by Markus Loewe and Esther Schüring, 1–35. Cheltenham, UK and Northampton, MA, USA: Edward Elgar Publishing.

Martela, F., B. Greve, B. Rothstein, and J. Saari. 2020. "The Nordic Exceptionalism: What Explains Why the Nordic Countries Are Constantly among the Happiest in the World." In *World Happiness Report, 2020*, edited by Jan Emmanuel De Neve John Helliwell, Richard Layard, and Jeffrey D. Sachs. New York: Sustainable Development Solutions Network. https://worldhappiness.report/ed/2020/#read, accessed 8 December 2021.

Morel, Nathalie, Chloé Touzet, and Michaël Zemmour. 2018. "Fiscal Welfare in Europe: Why Should We Care and What Do We Know so Far?" *Journal of European Social Policy* 28 (5): 549–60. https://doi.org/10.1177/0958928718802553.

Sinfield, A. 2019. "Fiscal Welfare." In *The Routledge Handbook of the Welfare State*, edited by B. Greve, 2nd edn, 23–33. Oxon: Routledge.

Wilson, Shaun. 2021. *Living Wages and the Welfare State: The Anglo-American Social Model in Transition*. Bristol: Policy Press.

9.   In-kind benefits – the service of the public sector

9.1   INTRODUCTION

Where in-cash benefits were central in the first few years in many societies, services have been of increasing importance in many countries for various reasons, but mainly as an expression that if left to the market, there would be a more limited supply of services than socially desired, combined with the fact that it could lead to a significant degree of inequality in the access to these services.

In addition, these areas affect the individual's social and economic security. At the same time as being economic investments, for example, education and care of children have the character of social investments, which can contribute to society on a number of parameters, which are then enabled to function better than they would otherwise. Explanations of why the public sector finances these areas vary, but basically it is largely based on a merit good argument in conjunction with the fact that collective solutions can be socially cheaper than individual solutions. Naturally, one will also need to discuss whether financing and producing the goods and services are connected, and how there can be different choices, including the use of user charges as a way of making users indicate preferences for the different areas.

The criteria for access, encompassing the available criteria and those actually used, are presented in Table 9.1 in the following section.

Childcare, even if it is a relatively new welfare service in many countries, is important for society for a number of reasons, which is central to Section 9.3. Section 9.4 then takes a closer look at healthcare, including why it is universal in most countries and a few words on user charges, including also what can be given as the main explanation for the change in spending on healthcare.

Education is then the focus of Section 9.5, including why education is provided, at least primary education, by the state and not the market, also by reference to human capital development. Labour market policy is a central public sector policy area in many countries. The active labour market policy (ALMP) is the focus in Section 9.6.

Then in Section 9.7, long-term care, especially for the elderly, is central, but this does not underestimate the fact that, for example, people with disabilities need social services in order to be able to live a life as close to normal as others can.

Section 9.8 concludes the chapter.

9.2   CRITERIA FOR ACCESS TO IN-KIND BENEFITS

In Table 9.1 below is shown possible criteria for access to in-kind benefits. They vary from country to country and do thereby not indicate that they are exhaustive.

Table 9.1   *Possible criteria for access to in-kind benefits in welfare states*

	In-kind
Age	Access to leisure activities
Unemployed	Training and/or education in some countries
Need	Long-term care
	Day-care
Sick	Hospitals
Low income	Cheaper/free health services
Non-work ability/people with disabilities	Different kind of help remedies and services to participate in societal activities

Source: Own depiction.

Table 9.1 is a clear indication of the variation of possible criteria for access to and conditions related to having access to several services. Where some can be objective indicators (age, sick, disabilities, unemployed, income) others can be more difficult (e.g. need but also the degree of work-ability). The possible in-kind benefits can also vary but show at the same time that the public sector can have a role in a large variety of services. Even if access to these services this might be combined with user charges and/or the level of services available.

9.3   DAY-CARE FOR CHILDREN

Day-care for children has been a growing activity in many developed countries over the last 15–20 years, and it started even earlier in the Nordic welfare states.

Day-care for children can be argued to have two important societal effects:

(1)   It provides the opportunity to support children's social, cognitive, etc. development (see also Chapter 11 on social investment).
(2)   It allows both parties to be in the labour market (where many countries previously only had a male breadwinner system).

Day-care for children is an example of a service that could, and has in some countries to a large extent been, in principle be well provided by the market, although due to the price of the service there could be a risk that many would not be able to pay. This or the total combined marginal tax and benefit rate would be very high, that is, there would be no economic incentive to work (this is also discussed in Chapter 8). This will especially be the case if the user charge is very high.

The need to provide day-care does not in itself inform about the quality and the price the public sector will charge for it, but it is a service where if left to the market, the total supply will be too low from an overall societal viewpoint.

9.4   HEALTHCARE

Health is central to most people and their experience of having a good life. There is by now an abundant number of books and articles on health, health-care and health economics, which have inspired this section. In addition, they all give more details than it is possible to do within the limits of this book (see e.g. Getzen 2010; Donaldson 2011; Devaux 2015; Drummond et al. 2015; Folland, Goodman, and Stano 2016). There are many and varied ways of financing healthcare, and the systems used vary widely in different countries (Paris et al. 2016; Reibling, Ariaans, and Wendt 2019; Tikkanen et al. 2020).

Health is often described in the literature as a luxury good, meaning that the elasticity of demand is above 1, which means that when a person or society becomes richer, the demand for treatment increases. However, some recent studies indicate that it is more frequently around 0.75 (i.e. a necessity good) (Marino et al. 2017), albeit there are also other pressures on spending. This implies that there is an ongoing pressure for higher levels of spending within healthcare. In the word "luxury" there are no assumptions about the quality of the service, only that it, theoretically, should imply a demand for a larger amount of health services is desired when we become richer.

Conversely, this does not mean in relation to individual elements within healthcare that there cannot be a connection as usual in the product market. If the price of a medicine rises, all other things being equal, it will lead to a decrease in the demand for the medicine in question. However, it will depend on whether there are other medicines with the same effect present at a lower price, and also because some medicine is a life necessity. This can also be influenced by who is financing the medicine. The connection may be greater if it is the individual who has to pay than if it is the state and/or an insurance company.

The principal–agent issue (as discussed in Chapter 7) is also of central importance for understanding the interaction in the field of health between the state, the market and the users, but also the relationship between the individual suppliers and the users is interesting. There are many and very different intersections within the health area which contribute to the fact that it is complicated to analyse financially, as well as to administer the area, including also where the expenses and expenditure development can be managed in the best possible way.

9.4.1   Some Core Concepts

There are a number of concepts that it is necessary to have an understanding of when analysing the development within the healthcare area. These are presented in more detail in this section. The concepts are central in order to be able to analyse and also understand the challenges of managing and prioritizing within the healthcare area.

One important concept is QALY (Quality Adjusted Life Years). It tries to assess the quality of life, which can be calculated from a number of methods that look at both physical and mental health, for example, EQ-5D. This is then multiplied by the number of years the individual is expected to have left to live, that is, remaining life-expectancy. It can be criticized for being difficult to calculate, including how quality is understood and how reliable its measurement can be. The scale is from 1 to 0 (dead). Thus, the higher the better.

Another is DALY (Disability free Adjusted Life Years) that tries to measure the number of years in which the individual lives without various kinds of obstacles in living a life as close to normal as others can.

These can then be linked to a third concept, WTP (Willingness to Pay), which indicates how much the individual or society is willing to pay to improve the state of health, for example, through medical or surgical treatment. What the individual is willing to pay can be difficult to measure. This is because the preferences of individuals are different, but also the economic conditions of the person in question can have an influence on the level of this. Therefore, the concept is most useful to ensure awareness that there may be a need to assess costs and benefits to each other (cf. also the section on the analysis of how resources are used in the best possible way). It might also be the case that one tries to estimate the shadow price of health, which also is difficult. One study indicated that a QALY in Australia using a method where life-satisfaction was included would be between 42,000 and 67,000 Australian dollars (Huang et al. 2018). Using different methods to estimate the economic value of benefits by intervention is difficult, and therefore it is also important to be open and transparent about the way it has been done, as it can influence the decision on whether or not to use new treatments, including medicine.

A separate problem in the health field is that there may be provider-induced demand, that is, the healthcare provider can increase the demand for its own services. This means that professionals can, for example, ask a patient to come back for an extra examination or more treatments than may be necessary because of differences in information between the provider and the person in need of treatment, as well as possible uncertainty about the exact health condition. Theoretically, this is known to exist, but it can be difficult to document (see e.g. Richardson and Peacock 2006). In any case, it implies a need to check that no unnecessary treatments are carried out or too much is charged for activities performed.

Diagnosis-related group (DRG) is a concept where the cost of each diagnosis is estimated and then used as payment to the provider for the specific treatment. Principally, this is an easy way to allocate resources, and should imply incentives for providers to change the cost of the provision so that the average cost of the treatment equals the DRG price. However, given it is difficult to have full details of all treatments within a DRG system, a risk is that providers try to argue that it was a more complicated treatment or that there were multiple diagnoses to be paid for.

A risk related hereto is the concept of cream-skimming, which implies that especially private providers will try to have only the easiest patients as they can be treated at a lower cost and still get the higher DRG rate, as already argued a long time ago (Ellis 1998) implying a higher surplus. Ellis also argued that skimping is a risk, which is when the quality of the treatment is of a lower quality than what is paid for. Dumping is a related concept where the provider argues that they can't treat a patient.

9.4.2 Spending on Healthcare and Possible Explanations for the Development

In the following, we first look at what the expenditure on health is like and how high it is in a number of European countries in particular, and then we look at possible drivers for change in expenditure within the area, as this can help to ensure knowledge of possible future expenditure developments, but also that it contributes to clarifications of whether and how much there is a willingness to pay for. Lastly, we look at how to measure the development within the health area, including not only expenses, but also productivity and other indicators of the development, such as life-expectancy.

In the field of health, most European countries have universalism, understood in the sense that if a person becomes acutely ill, there is the possibility of treatment regardless of whether or not an insurance has been taken out. This does not mean that there can be no requirement for self-payment, for example, when visiting a general practitioner or when buying medicine, or that everyone has easy access to all types of healthcare treatment.

Figure 9.1 shows the expenditure on healthcare as a proportion of GDP in 2012 and 2019. One possible problem with these types of data is that they are influenced by different developments across countries, and one thus needs to be aware hereof. A further problem is that in some countries expenditures in relation to long-term care are also included. Therefore, one needs to be cautious about interpreting the data, but the development over time can still be shown.

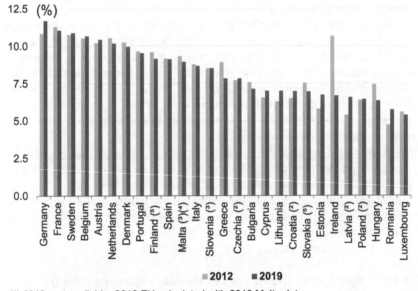

(¹) 2012: not available. 2019 EU calculated with 2018 Malta data
(²) 2013 instead of 2012.
(³) 2014 instead of 2012.
(⁴) 2018 instead of 2019.
(⁵) Break in series.

Source: Data from https://ec.europa.eu/eurostat/statistics-explained/index.php?title= Healthcare_expenditure_statistics#Healthcare_expenditure, accessed 17 December 2021.

Figure 9.1   *Current healthcare expenditure relative to GDP, 2012 and 2019 (%)*

The figure is an indication of two specific issues:

(a)   Spending is typically higher in the Northern and Western parts of Europe than in the Eastern and Southern parts.

(b)   Changes since 2012 have been relatively limited – some up and some down – with a large decline in Ireland as the exception.

Still, overall it is an indication that spending on healthcare is a high share of GDP, and thereby also as a large part of the overall government spending in all countries. This increases the need for knowing how to steer the spending, to manage the resources most efficiently and be aware of possible future pressure on the overall level of government spending. At the same time, there has been slower growth in spending in recent years compared to earlier (Lorenzoni et al. 2017).

In order to have a more precise picture, it is important to have the data in fixed prices to avoid the impact of inflation when analysing the development in spending, as well as taking into consideration the size of population. This is done in Table 9.2 when calculating the development in spending since 2000 in EU member states, as well as the level of spending per person in 2019.

Table 9.2 shows that, measured in fixed prices per inhabitant, in all EU countries there has been an increase since 2000; however, if using data from 2008 to 2018 there have been reductions in four countries in Southern Europe. An indicator is that if arguing that there has been austerity in a welfare state, one needs to clearly show the time used for the analysis (Greve 2020). At the same time, the table reveals that the largest increase in spending in the last 20 years has been in the countries with the, also still, lowest level of spending per inhabitant, implying a narrowing of the gap in spending between countries, albeit to a limited extent. The highest levels of spending can be found in the Western and Northern parts of Europe, and conversely the lowest level in Eastern and Southern Europe.

Overall, there are a number of drivers, these include: "demographic factors, rising incomes, technological progress, productivity in the healthcare sector compared to the general economy (Baumol's cost disease) and associated healthcare policies" (Marino et al. 2017). Thus, there are factors, assuming there is no change in quality, that are outside the scope of political decisions, implying that ageing and productivity can be argued to influence only costs, whereas income, technology and policy might also be used to improve quality and/or access to services. Technology is included as this is a factor that might both reduce or expand the cost of delivering healthcare. Increases due to new technology, which includes not only machines, but also new types of medicine, might be costly, while at the same time they might be more effective and, for example, reduce the time needed at a hospital.

Baumol's cost disease refers to the fact that as wages in the public sector often follow development in the private sector, then without necessarily the

Table 9.2   *Percentage change in spending on sickness/healthcare*
                 2008–18 and 2000–2019 in fixed prices per inhabitant and
                 level in 2018 or 2019

	2008–18	2000–19	Level in 2018 or 2019
EU-28	18.5%		2 248 45
Belgium	2.8%	31.7%	2 674 73
Bulgaria (2005)	56.3%	113.0%	364 00
Czechia (2018)	23.5%	58.7%	1 066 42
Denmark	3.9%	40.5%	3 177 60
Germany	42.8%	56.7%	3 812 44
Estonia	25.9%	148.4%	756 13
Ireland	12.1%	88.8%	3 330 39
Greece (2018)	-39.1%	8.3%	842 46
Spain	-9.4%	30.3%	1 552 31
France	14.2%	34.9%	3 043 68
Croatia (2008)	19.3%	26.3%	902 67
Italy	-5.5%	17.5%	1 766 60
Cyprus	-18.2%	54.9%	1 131 09
Latvia	38.3%	318.2%	573 55
Lithuania	30.6%	191.5%	704 25
Luxembourg	12.6%	56.6%	4 796 59
Hungary	7.5%	46.5%	629 86
Malta	37.4%	90.5%	1 282 99
Netherlands	10.1%	66.2%	3 873 92
Austria	9.4%	28.7%	2 851 08
Poland	33.7%	175.3%	665 14
Portugal	5.2%	22.6%	1 172 52
Romania	69.5%	365.0%	434 51
Slovenia	12.5%	54.5%	1 567 84
Slovakia (2018)	30.4%	50.2%	835 64
Finland	1.3%	39.9%	2 555 45
Sweden	14.1%	25.9%	3 250 60
UK (2018)	23.8%	77.4%	2 743 37

Note: The year shown in parentheses after country names indicates whether either the first or last year available deviates from the other countries. As can be seen for six countries, data for all years 2000–19 are not available.
Source: Eurostat, [SPR_EXP_FSI__custom_1454705], accessed 23 October 2021 and calculations based hereupon.

same increase in productivity as in the private sector, the wage increase can imply a higher cost of providing healthcare (Baumol 1967). In principle, this can also be the case in other parts of the welfare states, and is also part of the ongoing discussion and analysis of how to provide benefits and services as efficiently as possible.

9.4.3 How to Produce Effectively, Prioritize and Steer within the Health Area

One important issue is to know the many and varied drivers of, which mainly increases spending, in the cost of healthcare, and further that in the more affluent countries there is constantly a demand for more services. This includes how to figure out by what means to assess and decide to invest in new areas, as well as the importance of steering the overall change in spending. There can be a number of ways to manage the economic consequences of the demand for healthcare.

With the exception of acute illness and needing urgent treatment, using waiting lists and waiting times in most countries for when a person can be treated is a way of reducing the demand as well as using the scarce resources most effectively. The economic explanation for this is that if any disease is to be treated immediately, it would require a very large capacity, and thus also that in periods when there are not so many in need of treatment there will be excess capacity. The balance will constantly be a professional assessment of what can be postponed without major risk to the citizen and what cannot. In addition, it will be very expensive (due to periods of excess capacity) to avoid waiting times for certain treatments, just as it is possible that there may be a risk of insufficiently qualified staff being available all the time, and thus optimal utilization of labour might require waiting lists and, dependent on the type of disease, the length of acceptable waiting times.

Another option to reduce the financial pressure on health is by trying to prevent bad health, for example, by nudging people towards a healthier life-style, that is, trying to reduce unhealthy nutrition, smoking and high alcohol consumption, as well as to increase physical activity. Prevention also includes screening for possible diseases (e.g. some types of cancer) as well as vaccination, most recently witnessed in the COVID-19 crisis, but also for long-term vaccination of children against certain diseases, which also might have positive externalities on the situation for other children.

Of course, prevention cannot eliminate all diseases, but it may contribute to what is called healthy ageing, which means that even though we live longer, we have healthier life years, that is, more DALY. We know that prevention not only in healthcare, but also more broadly in social policy, can be important, albeit it is not always clear whether it is cost-effective as there might also be costs related to preventative initiatives (Berghman, Debels, and Van Hoyweghen 2019). Still, it can improve life-quality, as well as enabling a possible higher labour supply. How to measure all elements in a cost-benefit or cost-effectiveness analysis might be difficult. Prevention might also help in healthy ageing and thereby reduce the pressure on healthcare cost as a consequence of the demographic changes.

In the market, price is a factor that regulates the demand for goods and services. In the healthcare market, it is theoretically possible to charge user fees to regulate demand. Such fees are usually not present when in need of being treated urgently, but in a number of countries there is a payment when visiting the general practitioner. The argument for this is, as in the general market, that it should help users to consider whether it is necessary to go to the doctor. One risk here is that some come "too late" to the doctor, and thus that a disease has developed to a more serious stage and, perhaps, is even fatal. If this is the case, the user fee may have entailed greater expenses than otherwise for treatment in the health system. There are many different ways to have user payments that may help to reduce this risk by, for example, exempting people with modest incomes from payment, or by having a maximum to pay within a year, or persons with chronic diseases being exempted from payments. Overall, it illustrates a trade-off of managing aggregate demand with the risk that the cost of treatment for some will grow.

In many countries, there are also user fees for medicines and services from, for example, dentists, physiotherapists, and so on. User fees mean in this context that there are some, for example, people with income below the poverty line, who cannot afford to buy the necessary medicine, which can contribute to inequality in health. Thereby, user payments also become an instrument which, on the one hand, can contribute to regulating demand and thereby the overall level of public expenditure on healthcare, but which, on the other hand, has the consequence that it can increase inequality in a society.

Arguing that people need to take out a private healthcare insurance as a way of then paying for treatment can also be a way of steering the expenditures. How the total cost is distributed between insurance companies, the individual and the state depends on the tax system (tax expenditures; see Morel, Touzet, and Zemmour 2018; Sinfield 2019). If payment to an insurance company or other ways to pay for health care is deductible, this will imply that the state, by getting lower income from taxation, thereby pays, albeit indirectly, part of the costs.

There are economically a number of possible problems of using insurance as a way of financing.

The first is the risk of moral hazard. Moral hazard is when those who have insurance have a lesser incentive to behave rationally. Whether it is a fire insurance or health insurance, for example, it may be that the behaviour to reduce the risk of fire or to become ill is reduced. How big the problem is in the healthcare field can be difficult to document, as there is hardly anyone who consciously wants to get sick. To the extent that the welfare state is considered an insurance, there is the same risk that it affects incentives for sensible behaviour, such as exercising too little or smoking too much.

Adverse selection, which is a form of market failure, is also a problem, and can make it difficult to apply insurance policies. This is because the same information is not available to both the insurance provider and its claimants. It is possible, as when shopping for other goods, that there is a bad piece among the fruit you buy. Or in other words, someone who does not reveal all his risks of needing extensive healthcare can become costly for the insurance company. The company will, of course, try to avoid this. This can be done through screening of applicants, but there is then a risk that for "bad" lives it gets harder to take out insurance or that the premium for the insurance will be so high that many cannot affod to take it out, and thus that some in an insurance system would be at risk of not receiving treatment. In addition, companies may try to cream-skim so that their profits can be maximized. This can be avoided in a common public system in what Barr has, for a long time, called a piggy bank (Barr 2001).

Lastly, there is a high risk that the transaction costs will be high, including because there must be screening of insurance holders, it must be checked that the producers do not deliver more treatments than necessary, and so on. The latter will also be needed in a public system. But, overall, there are many indications that transaction costs are lower in a public sector than in an insurance-based healthcare system (Donaldson 2011).

Overall, co-financing including out-of-pocket payments is an important part of financing healthcare, while also an instrument to help in trying to manage the demand for healthcare, and thereby reduce the pressure on public expenditure. Several of these instruments tend to have an upside-down effect with regard to the impact on the distribution in societies.

Table 9.3 shows the out-of-pocket payments for healthcare as part of the total cost on health in a number of OECD countries, along with their development since 2010 in selected years.

As can be witnessed from the table, there is large variation ranging from below 10 per cent to close to 40 per cent. Payments include elements such as visiting general practitioners, paying for medicine, dentist, physiotherapy, and so on. The elements the users have to pay for can vary across countries. The relatively low level in the US can be explained by user charges being paid by insurance (either private or paid by employers). The development has, in most countries, been at a standstill or even in decline, albeit in a few countries there has been an increase. Still, out-of-pocket payment is an important part of the

Table 9.3   *Out-of-pocket payments for healthcare as a proportion of*
                   total cost in selected OECD countries since 2010

Year	2010	2013	2016	2019	2020
Country					
Austria	18.6	19.2	19.2	17.7	16.9
Belgium	20.0	19.6	18.0	18.2	
Czech Republic	15.3	13.6	15.0	14.2	
Denmark	14.4	13.8	13.7	14.2	
Estonia	21.9	22.6	22.7	23.9	20.4
Finland	18.8	17.8	19.3	17.4	
France	10.2	9.9	9.6	9.3	
Germany	13.8	13.2	12.9	12.7	12.3
Greece	28.3	34.1	34.9	35.2	
Hungary	27.4	28.4	27.7	28.2	
Ireland	13.8	14.3	12.8	11.7	10.6
Italy	20.5	22.2	23.3	23.3	21.1
Lithuania	27.6	32.8	32.3	32.3	32.3
Latvia	37.2	38.5	43.3	37.1	
Luxembourg	10.2	11.2	10.7	9.6	
Netherlands	9.1	11.5	11.3	10.6	9.5
Norway	15.0	14.6	14.3	13.9	13.7
Poland	23.7	23.6	22.8	20.1	19.5
Portugal	24.7	28.8	29.4	30.5	26.4
Slovak Republic	22.8	23.3	18.2	19.2	
Slovenia	12.6	12.5	12.0	11.7	10.1
Spain	20.3	22.8	22.0	21.8	
Sweden	16.4	14.9	14.5	13.9	13.7
Switzerland	26.2	25.2	26.6	25.3	
United Kingdom	13.0	15.2	15.4	15.9	13.8
United States	12.4	12.3	11.6	11.3	

Source: https://stats.oecd.org/viewhtml.aspx?datasetcode=SHA&lang=en, accessed 2 October
2021.

financing in many countries. This also implies that a number of people in each
country can't afford the necessary treatment, including paying for medicine.

Table 9.4   *Five-year survival rates for breast cancer in a number of OECD countries*

	Breast cancer five year net survival		
	Female		
	2000–04	2005–09	2010–14
Country			
Austria	81.7	83.9	84.8
Belgium	84.8	85.3	86.4
Czech Republic	75.7	79.1	81.4
Denmark	80.3	84.0	86.1
Estonia	71.1	75.4	78.1
Finland	86.5	87.7	88.5
France	86.8	87.2	86.7
Germany	83.9	85.6	86.0
Ireland	77.2	81.4	82.0
Italy	84.2	85.9	86.0
Lithuania	64.6	71.3	73.5
Latvia	69.3	73.3	76.9
Netherlands	83.9	85.8	86.6
Poland	71.3	74.7	76.5
Portugal	81.6	86.1	87.6
Slovak Republic	75.3	76.6	75.5
Slovenia	78.7	82.5	83.5
Spain	82.9	84.6	85.3
Sweden	85.6	87.9	88.8
United Kingdom	79.8	83.8	85.6
United States	88.9	89.8	90.2

Note: Rates are age standardized for those above the age of 15.
Source: Health Statistics – OECD, accessed 17 December 2021.

Overall, how to produce effectively also includes the use of best practice and evidence, thus evidence-based steering (see more in Section 7.3) is an important element related to prioritization within healthcare.

Naturally, a specific element includes the more ethical issues, because it is most likely that intervention for the young will give a higher return in QALY than treatment of the elderly. Still, evidence can be used to compare different interventions for the same age groups, including also whether, for example, new medicine is cost-effective compared to the existing medicine on the market for a treatment.

It is difficult to measure productivity within the healthcare sector for a number of reasons, including that different treatments may take different times and the quantity of operations, for example, can vary, which is highly dependent on the development in sickness. New technology might also, as an example, imply that a patient can be discharged faster. This will imply a lower number of days at hospital and can be considered an improved productivity. However, typically, this increase cannot be expected to be the same for future years. However, a simple measure would be the number of full-time staff related to the number of activities done within the healthcare system.

Another indicator, albeit not only as a consequence of the activities in the healthcare sector, is the average life-expectancy. One can also look into how long a time after, for example, a cancer diagnosis a patient can be expected to be alive, which can also be seen as a quality indicator. This is shown in Table 9.4.

The table shows different developments and increases in all countries except France, and the largest increase in countries with a lower rate than others in 2000–04 such as Lithuania and Latvia. The improvement in survival rates is also part of the increase in life-expectancy seen in many countries, which in Figure 9.2 is for those above the age of 65.

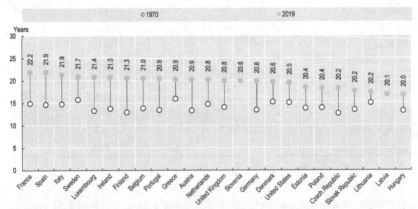

Source: *Health at a Glance* (2021), Paris: OECD (Life expectancy and healthy life expectancy at age 65): OECD Indicators | OECD iLibrary (oecd-ilibrary.org).

Figure 9.2   *Life-expectancy at age 65, 1970 and 2019 (or nearest year) in a number of OECD countries*

Figure 9.2 shows that in all countries those reaching the age of 65 will on average have more than 20 years still to live. This is an increase of around five years since 1970 in all countries, which is also due partly to the healthcare system, and partly the better living conditions. This is an indicator that there are demographic changes underway that imply a pressure on the public sector (this is returned to in Chapter 12).

9.5   EDUCATION

Education is a key element in most societies' development. The role of the public sector here is also very strong in most societies. There are a number of reasons for this.

Firstly, without public sector involvement, there would probably be fewer people taking an education, and is thus an example of a merit good argument for a society to intervene, implying a lower level of human capital. Human capital is the individual personal capabilities, such as skills, talent and knowledge. They can be acquired by education, but also on-the-job experience can have an impact. Human capital theory was developed especially by Gary Becker (1985).

The merit good argument is especially used in relation to primary education. This is because without public sector intervention a number of children would not go to school, and would not be able, at the very least, to read and write. There are different traditions for the extent of public intervention in relation to higher education, as well as continuing and further education. Still, overall, public intervention thus helps to ensure a high level of human capital.

Secondly, human capital is an important parameter for a country's competitiveness, including in relation for the individual to be able to have a job in the short and long term, and also that education might increase productivity in societies.

Theoretically, there could be a market for education, and if there was a well-functioning capital market then students (or their parents) would be able to borrow to pay for education, given that on average lifetime income is higher for people with education than for people without, and thereby enabling them to pay back the loan. But whether everyone would then take out a loan would depend on the degree of risk the individual is willing to take, and risk aversion will be higher for some than for others, carrying the risk that fewer people than the optimum for society will get an education. Therefore, the third reason why the state intervenes is because it increases allocative efficiency.

Fourthly, it can be argued that the fact that more people have a qualifying education contributes to a positive externality, as education, in addition to contributing to a greater extent to being able to get a job, also to a greater extent contributes to democratic and economic equality. Thus, education and ensuring the necessary qualifications for the labour force is also an important element with regard to having the necessary competence to be able to take up new types of job, given the constant technological development and ongoing changes on the labour market (see more in Section 9.6).

At the same time, there are also good reasons for societies to invest in research, as research can help in ensuring a higher level of qualifications, but also because, given the possible high risk of obtaining results and the ability to earn money from research, this implies a need for societies to step in. Further, also, as results from public-supported research imply a positive externality in the sense that the knowledge will then, normally, be available for everyone in society. This is in contrast to privately funded research, such as in the medical sector, as those paying for the research due to the high cost of spending when developing new products often have a patent for ten years.

9.6   ACTIVE LABOUR MARKET POLICY

The labour market is central for many reasons. Labour is a factor of production, which in many and different areas contributes to the production of a country, just as capital and land do. But the labour market is also the place where many people earn their income, and for many this is an important part of having social contacts, to be able to use their skills and contribute to the development of society.

The price in the labour market for labour is the wage. Theoretically, the price is formed in the labour market in the same way as in the commodity market, that is, there is a connection between supply and demand for labour, including that the individual's wage depends on productivity, although this can often be difficult to measure for the individual. In reality, there is not only a labour market, but also in all countries a number of different labour markets depending on, for example, geography, education, and so on.

At the same time, there are a number of institutional restrictions as a result of a number of rules that regulate the labour market in most countries. This applies, for example, to health and safety in the workplace, including the need for rest and how many hours may be worked during a day. But in addition, in many countries there is a legal statutory minimum wage that must be paid. In other countries, the minimum wage is part of the collective agreements in the labour market. The following is divided into two subsections: (1) Unemployment and employment and (2) Active labour market policies

9.6.1   Unemployment and Employment

There are various theoretical explanations for the fact that there is unemployment and how it changes over time.

One is based on the fact that people are unemployed because they are not willing to accept the ongoing wages on the labour market based on the qualifications they have. In this understanding, unemployment is thus voluntary and not something that society must intervene in and try to adjust. It is the neoclassical understanding of unemployment where there will be equilibrium in the labour market (including the price of labour (wages)), implying that supply and demand meet. This is also part of the debate on economic incentives to take up a job (see more in Chapter 8).

The other, which can to a large extent be described as Keynesian, focuses more on the significance of total demand for the extent of unemployment, without neglecting, however, that wages will have an effect on how many people will also be employed in the long term.

In a neoclassical sense, the market will by itself solve the problem of employment and unemployment, and there is therefore no need for the government to intervene.

In a Keynesian understanding, unemployment could be affected through changes in the extent of aggregate demand.

There are therefore also different forms and understandings of unemployment. Unemployment can be changed due to the business cycle, new technology, seasonal changes and unemployment when being between jobs.

Business cyclical unemployment is about the fact that the total economic activity can vary over time, and even be affected by external crises, such as the financial crisis. In periods of high economic activity (and thus high level of employment) there will be few unemployed, and in periods of low economic activity there will be more unemployed. The extent of this will vary from country to country.

Seasonal unemployment means that within a number of industries (e.g. tourism and construction) there is variation in demand, and some will therefore have a greater risk of being unemployed during certain periods of the year.

The development in technology also has an impact on not necessarily only the total number of jobs available, but at least in which areas more or less labour is needed. Historically, several types of jobs have disappeared and new ones have been added (see e.g. Arntz, Gregory, and Zierahn 2016; Schwab 2016; Greve 2017; Peralta-Alva and Roitman 2018; Georgieff and Milanez 2021). But even if it does not mean changes in the number of jobs, it can have an influence on where the jobs are and what competencies are needed to be able to solve the various tasks, and thus also what types of support the public sector can help with, in order to ensure a better connection between demand and supply of labour.

There is a distinction between active and passive labour market policy. The focus in this chapter is on active labour market policy (ALMP), whereas the passive one is dealt with in Chapter 8.

The opposite side of unemployment is employment. But at the same time, it is not only the salary that may have an effect on whether a person can find work. This is because there is a risk of discrimination in the labour market, for example, due to age, gender, ethnicity or disability. Here it can be difficult to distinguish between whether it is the provider of labour who will not accept the conditions in the labour market, or whether it is the employers as a result of bias in preferring others for the available jobs. We can see, for example, that migrants have a smaller connection to the labour market than others (Jurado and Brochmann 2013; Brochmann and Dølvik 2018), just as people with disabilities have jobs to a lesser extent than others. Similarly, the employment rate for women in most countries is still lower than for men, which has partly historical reasons, including the fact that childcare has only recently been offered by the public sector in a number of countries. Elderly people becoming unemployed also more often than others have difficulties in re-entering the labour market.

There are also groups who want to work full time, however, may only be able to get a part-time job, and are therefore underemployed. There are a number of groups in the labour market that have very precarious working conditions (Kreshpaj et al. 2020; Shin, Kemppainen, and Kuitto 2021), and often not with the same social rights as others. These may be, for example, persons who are considered self-employed (solo-self-employed) and they are not covered to the same extent as others by social security schemes (Palier 2019).

Changes in the direction of jobs that are available via a platform, or other new types of jobs (Spasova et al. 2021) and with great uncertainty about the scope and salary, contribute to more groups in the labour market having poorer wages and working conditions than other groups.

Historically, these differences have also been referred to as a distinction between insiders and outsiders (Doeringer and Piore 1971), or core and periphery workers (Lindbeck and Snower 1988), indicating that economic incentives and issues are not the only things at stake when one wants to explain the development on the labour market.

A description of differences between national labour markets is given here, but for Europe and a number of countries outside Europe, there is a lot of data to be obtained, for example, via Eurostat and the OECD.

Flexibility and security have been a desire for both employers and employees, with different emphases on what they find important. Employers want flexibility so that it is easy to hire and fire, whereas employees want security in employment, both through notice of termination and the opportunity to find a new job quickly if unemployed. In addition, there is financial security in connection with unemployment, for example, through unemployment benefits. The combination of flexibility and security is often referred to as flexi-curity (Tros and Wilthagen 2013; Bekker 2018). How the combination of safety and security varies from country to country depends on the welfare model, but in addition assessments of advantages and disadvantages, where it is argued that a long notice of termination causes employers to refrain from accepting permanent employment, and conversely that a shorter notice of termination causes more employees to want a higher financial compensation in case of unemployment. Long notice periods are also argued as an obstacle to flexible development in the labour market, but conversely that security in employment ensures better working conditions and production, as well as life satisfaction. In order to contribute to job security, there is also, to varying degrees, an ALMP across countries (cf. the next section).

9.6.2   Active Labour Market Policies

There has, at least since the 1950s, been discussions on ALMP, its contents and its aims. The OECD defines ALMP as:

> The objective of an effective activation policy is to give more people access to the labour force and good jobs. This requires:
>
> Enhancing motivation and incentives to seek employment.
> Improving job readiness and help in finding suitable employment.
> Expanding employment opportunities.
>
> The implementation of these key elements needs to be managed by effective and well-coordinated labour market and social institutions and policies. Continuous monitoring and evaluation of the impact of policies and programmes are necessary to strengthen policy effectiveness and efficiency in responding to the needs of different groups. (Active Labour Market Policies: Connecting People with Jobs – OECD, https://www.oecd.org/employment/activation.htm?msclkid=1f4eeef1b0c4 11ecac742a2c97682632, accessed 21 November 2021)

A further distinction is made between whether activation should be an aid to the development of human capital or work through a threat effect. Upgrading of qualifications aims to ensure that the unemployed gain the professional and social skills that make it possible to get a job in the labour market. This can also involve activation with wage subsidies, which contributes to the individual gaining work experience as the given wage rate and their competences might not enable them to get a job. The threat effect means that the activation is not attractive, and that the unemployed take any job regardless of content and salary. It is not possible to measure exactly which of the effects is most effective.

Overall, the assessment is that what works in the ALMP is activation in private companies and education in times of recession (Card, Kluve, and Weber 2018; Escudero 2018; Dinan 2019; Nordlund and Greve 2019; Knotz 2020), which is also confirmed in a number of analyses in the wake of COVID-19 (see the OECD's webpage hereabout https://www.oecd.org/els/

emp/activation.htm, accessed 23 November 2021). The reason why activation in private companies is more efficient is due to the greater probability of getting a job when the activation is over, as there are more job openings here than in the public sector. This is because most public institutions have tight budgets that typically only change once a year, whereas private companies can change if there is a greater demand for their goods and services. Education works in a recession as it prepares the unemployed for the jobs that will exist when there is more economic growth in the economy again. Similarly, when it does not work in a boom, it is because there are far more who return to the labour market quickly even after unemployment because there are many jobs to apply for. This is also one of the economic issues related to activation. If the unemployed would have got a job anyhow, then spending money on activation creates a deadweight loss. Thus, in order to be economically effective, activation should move the individual closer to or into the labour market, but not be spent on people who would anyhow and quickly get back to the labour market. Only empirical analysis of different kinds of interventions can show this (see also the studies mentioned above).

The fact that someone returns to the labour market quickly after unemployment is also an explanation for the fact that it is not appropriate to start activation until a person has been unemployed for some time. There has also been an increasing focus on being aware that, for some, the path to or back to the labour market is longer than others, and thus that the success criterion will not only be having or not having a job, but whether the person has moved closer to the labour market.

To be financially efficient, the ALMP should ensure that as many unemployed as possible in times of strong changes in the labour market, for example, as a result of new technology, are able and have the necessary competencies for new vacancies at the job market. At the same time, transaction costs should be as limited as possible. The better the match between employers' and employees' wishes is important as this might help with more efficient production and a stable attachment to the labour market.

9.7   LONG-TERM CARE

Long-term care is often understood as the care for persons in need of permanent help with basic issues due to physical or mental disability. This can therefore be wide ranging, such as help with a few basic daily issues, for example, cleaning, food and personal hygiene, to a permanent stay in an institution with support for most issues, including more personal care. Long-term care is thus not only for elderly people, but can also include others with different and typically permanent needs.

Long-term care is a good example of the economic reason for collective action, because if "the premium is based on the risk of an event occurring and the size of the resulting loss" (Barr 2010, 360), then it will only by pooling resources together be economically possible for individuals to be covered in case of need. This is because the problem is that no one knows whether or not they will need long-term care.[1] If everyone takes out an insurance, then the transaction cost will be higher than if care is collectively financed. If everyone saves in order, in principle, to be able to pay in case need arises, then this will imply a very high saving rate with the risk of reducing the demand for goods and services.

Perhaps for the above-mentioned reasons, private insurance seems not to have been used to a large extent by citizens. This includes, further, the following central reasons: excessive costs, social assistance, trust in family solidarity, unattractive rules of reimbursement, ignorance and denial of heavy dependence (Pestieau and Ponthière 2012; Klimaviciute and Pestiau 2015). Overall, the insurance market for long-term care has not been developing (Costa-Font and Courbage 2015), which presumably also reflects the fact that in some welfare states part of the long-term care for the elderly has mainly been taken care of by the family or within the healthcare system, given the large diversity of long-term care in Europe (Greve 2019). Long-term care can thereby be argued to be one of the areas of the welfare state where, in principle, there could be a market. However, it could be more expensive than goods and services provided by a collective, reflecting the fact that the public sector can act as a piggy bank (Barr 2001).

There is also an issue about possible differences in equality with regard to access to services, as well as the impact on equality if the activities are left to the private market. A private market might also imply the use of hidden labour and migrant workers. Given the possible change in demography (see also Chapter 12), financing as well as ensuring the necessary labour force for long-term care is an issue for the public sector economy.

9.8   CONCLUDING REMARKS

Financing and the provision of a wide range of, and very different, services have become central in most countries for various reasons. There are, therefore, also a large and varied number of criteria for access to services, including variation in the way there are user charges.

Education, for example, is largely based on merit good arguments; care for the elderly on collective funding being more efficient than private funding; health as a result of the fact that many would otherwise not be treated and a greater degree of risk of inequality in access to services would then arise.

The ALMP is a contribution to a more efficient labour market and production in a society, but it can also be linked to the function of ensuring that the unemployed do not receive social benefits for too long.

Day-care for children also supports the labour supply, as well as giving the option for many to have both a working and a family life.

Naturally, services have to be financed and there must be choice and priorities between services, as well as between in-kind and in-cash benefits, which is a central issue in steering the public sector economy.

NOTE

1. Some are born with a need for long-term care or will be in need of long-term care for other reasons even before they reach the age where they have a chance to be on the labour market, but they will never be able to be insured or able to save for the cost of long-term care, and in these cases this will always be a task for the welfare state.

REFERENCES

Arntz, Melanie, Terry Gregory, and Ulrich Zierahn. 2016. "The Risk of Automation for Jobs in OECD Countries: A Comparative Analysis." 189. OECD Social, Employment and Migration Working Papers. Paris: OECD. https://doi.org/10.1787/5jlz9h56dvq7-en.

Barr, Nicholas. 2001. *The Welfare State as a Piggy Bank. Information, Risk, Uncertainty, and the Role of the State.* Oxford: Oxford University Press.

Barr, Nicholas. 2010. "Long-Term Care: A Suitable Case for Social Insurance." *Social Policy & Administration.* https://doi.org/10.1111/j.1467-9515.2010.00718.x.

Baumol, William J. 1967. "Macroeconomics of Unbalanced Growth: The Anatomy of Urban Crisis." *The American Economic Review* 57 (3): 415–26.

Becker, Gary S. 1985. "Human Capital, Effort, and the Sexual Division of Labor." *Journal of Labor Economics* 3 (1, Part 2): S33–58.

Bekker, Sonja. 2018. "Flexicurity in the European Semester: Still a Relevant Policy Concept?" *Journal of European Public Policy.* https://doi.org/10.1080/13501763.2017.1363272.

Berghman, J., A. Debels, and I. Van Hoyweghen. 2019. "Prevention: The Cases of Social Security and Healthcare." In *Routledge Handbook of the Welfare State*, edited by B. Greve, 2nd edn, 46–57. Oxon: Routledge.

Brochmann, Grete, and Jon Erik Dølvik. 2018. "The Welfare State and International Migration: The European Challenge". In *Routledge Handbook of the Welfare State*, edited by B. Greve, 508–22. Oxon: Routledge.

Card, David, Jochen Kluve, and Andrea Weber. 2018. "What Works? A Meta Analysis of Recent Active Labor Market Program Evaluations." *Journal of the European Economic Association.* https://doi.org/10.1093/jeea/jvx028.

Costa-Font, Joan, and Christophe Courbage. 2015. "Crowding out of Long-term Care Insurance: Evidence from European Expectations Data." *Health Economics* 24: 74–88.

Devaux, Marion. 2015. "Income-Related Inequalities and Inequities in Health Care Services Utilisation in 18 Selected OECD Countries." *The European Journal of Health Economics* 16 (1): 21–33.

Dinan, Shannon. 2019. "A Typology of Activation Incentives." *Social Policy & Administration* 53 (1): 1–15.

Doeringer, P., and M. Piore. 1971. *Internal Labor Markets and Manpower Analysis.* Lexington, KY: Health Lexington.

Donaldson, C. 2011. *Credit Crunch Health Care. How Economics Can Save Our Publicly Funded Health Services.* Bristol: Policy Press.

Drummond, Michael F., Mark J. Sculpher, Karl Claxton, Greg L. Stoddart, and George W. Torrance. 2015. *Methods for the Economic Evaluation of Health Care Programmes.* Oxford: Oxford University Press.

Ellis, Randall P. 1998. "Creaming, Skimping and Dumping: Provider Competition on the Intensive and Extensive Margins." *Journal of Health Economics* 17 (5): 537–55.

Escudero, Verónica. 2018. "Are Active Labour Market Policies Effective in Activating and Integrating Low-Skilled Individuals? An International Comparison." *IZA Journal of Labor Policy* 7 (1): 4.

Folland, Sherman, Allen Charles Goodman, and Miron Stano. 2016. *The Economics of Health and Health Care: Pearson New International Edition.* Oxon and New York: Routledge.

Georgieff, Alexandre, and Anna Milanez. 2021. "What Happened to Jobs at High Risk of Automation?" 255. OECD Social, Employment and Migration Working Papers. Paris: OECD.

Getzen, T. 2010. *Health Economics and Financing.* 4th edn. Hoboken, NJ: John Wiley & Sons.

Greve, B. 2017. *Technology and the Future of Work. The Impact on Labour Markets and Welfare States.* Cheltenham, UK and Northampton, MA, USA: Edward Elgar Publishing.

Greve, B. 2019. "Long-Term Care." In *Handbook of the Welfare State*, edited by B. Greve, 2nd edn, 498–507. Oxon: Routledge.

Greve, B. 2020. *Austerity, Retrenchment and the Welfare State. Truth or Fiction?* Cheltenham and and Northampton, MA, USA: Edward Elgar Publishing.

Huang, Li, Paul Frijters, Kim Dalziel, and Philip Clarke. 2018. "Life Satisfaction, QALYs, and the Monetary Value of Health." *Social Science & Medicine* 211: 131–6.

Jurado, Elena, and Grete Brochmann. 2013. *Europe's Immigration Challenge: Reconciling Work, Welfare and Mobility.* London: I.B. Tauris.

Klimaviciute, J., and P. Pestiau. 2015. "Long-Term Care Social Insurance: How to Avoid Big Losses?" *International Tax Public Finance* 25: 99–139. https://doi.org/10.1007/s10797-017+9445-5.

Knotz, Carlo Michael. 2020. "Does Demanding Activation Work? A Comparative Analysis of the Effects of Unemployment Benefit Conditionality on Employment in 21 Advanced Economies, 1980–2012." *European Sociological Review* 36 (1): 121–35.

Kreshpaj, Bertina, Cecilia Orellana, Bo Burström et al. 2020. "What Is Precarious Employment? A Systematic Review of Definitions and Operationalizations from Quantitative and Qualitative Studies." *Scandinavian Journal of Work, Environment & Health.*

Lindbeck, A., and D. Snower. 1988. *The Insider-Outsider Theory of Employment and Unemployment.* Cambridge, MA: MIT Press.

Lorenzoni, Luca, Jonathan Millar, Franco Sassi, and Douglas Sutherland. 2017. "Cyclical vs Structural Effects on Health Care Expenditure Trends in OECD Countries." 1507. OECD Economics Department Working Papers. Paris: OECD.

Marino, Alberto, David Morgan, Luca Lorenzoni, and Chris James. 2017. "Future Trends in Health Care Expenditure: A Modelling Framework for Cross-Country Forecasts." 95. OECD Health Working Papers. Paris: OECD.

Morel, Nathalie, Chloé Touzet, and Michaël Zemmour. 2018. "Fiscal Welfare in Europe: Why Should We Care and What Do We Know so Far?" *Journal of European Social Policy* 28 (5): 549–60. https://doi.org/10.1177/0958928718802553.

Nordlund, M., and B. Greve. 2019. "Focus on Active Labour Market Policies." In *The Routledge Handbook of the Welfare State*, edited by B. Greve, 2nd edn, 366–77. Oxon: Routledge.

Palier, Bruno. 2019. "Work, Social Protection and the Middle Classes: What Future in the Digital Age?" *International Social Security Review* 72 (3): 113–33. https://doi .org/10.1111/issr.12218.

Paris, V., E. Hewlett, J. Auraaen, and L. Simon. 2016. "Health Care Coverage in OECD Countries in 2012." 88. Health Working Papers. Paris: OECD.

Peralta-Alva, A., and A. Roitman. 2018. "Technology and the Future of Work." WP/18/207. IMF Working Paper.

Pestieau, Pierre, and Grégory Ponthière. 2012. "Long-Term Care Insurance Puzzle." In *Financing Long-Term Care in Europe*, 41–52. New York: Springer.

Reibling, Nadine, Mareike Ariaans, and Claus Wendt. 2019. "Worlds of Healthcare: A Healthcare System Typology of OECD Countries." *Health Policy* 123 (7): 611–20.

Richardson, Jeffrey R.J., and Stuart J. Peacock. 2006. "Supplier-Induced Demand." *Applied Health Economics and Health Policy* 5 (2): 87–98.

Schwab, K. 2016. *The Fourth Industrial Revolution*. Davos: World Economic Forum.

Shin, Young-Kyu, Teemu Kemppainen, and Kati Kuitto. 2021. "Precarious Work, Unemployment Benefit Generosity and Universal Basic Income Preferences: A Multilevel Study on 21 European Countries." *Journal of Social Policy* 50 (2): 323–45.

Sinfield, A. 2019. "Fiscal Welfare." In *The Routledge Handbook of the Welfare State*, edited by B. Greve, 2nd edn, 23–33. Oxon: Routledge.

Spasova, Slavina, Dalila Ghailani, Sebastiano Sabato, Stéphanie Coster, Boris Fronteddu, and Bart Vanhercke. 2021. "Non-Standard Workers and the Self-Employed in the EU: Social Protection during the Covid-19 Pandemic." *ETUI Research Paper – Report*.

Tikkanen, Roosa, Robin Osborn, Elias Mossialos, Ana Djordjevic, and George Wharton. 2020. "International Profiles of Health Care Systems." Technical Report, The Commonwealth Fund. https://www.researchgate.net/profile/Adriano -Massuda-2/publication/352750082_The_Brazilian_Health_Care_System/links/ 60d63a1e299bf1ea9ebe48df/The-Brazilian-Health-Care-System.pdf, accessed 10 December 2021.

Tros, F., and T. Wilthagen. 2013. "Flexicurity: Concepts, Practices, and Outcomes." In *The Routledge Handbook of the Welfare State*, edited by B. Greve, 1st edn, 125–35. Oxon: Routledge.

10. International influence, including the Economic and Monetary Union

10.1 INTRODUCTION

The economy of the public sector is affected not only by the development of the individual nation state including political decisions on the spending and level of taxes and duties, but also by the international economic development – often labelled globalization and/or regionalization – which can have an impact on the level of employment and possible tax revenue. The stronger possible impact from neighbouring countries is also the reason to have a focus mainly on the European development.

This chapter looks into the consequences of both financing and choice of consumption expenses and investments in infrastructure given the more open economies. The possible influence on the ability to ensure income from taxes and duties in a global world is presented in Section 10.2. The focus is on the impact of globalization, but also the possible restrictions on national abilities to decide on the economic policy, including the ability to decide on national levels of taxation.

In Section 10.3, there is a special focus on the countries covered by the Economic and Monetary Union (EMU) within the European Union (EU), where a closer look is taken at how the rules herein can influence the development of the public sector, and as well as a discussion of the logics of the rules. The requirements and size of the general government budget deficit and debt impact on the general government sector are discussed in Section 10.4. Section 10.5 then looks into how the global functioning of markets and economies can create options, but also reduce the degree of freedom to finance the public sector, including tax competition. Section 10.6 sums up the content of the chapter.

10.2 GLOBALIZATION, REGIONALIZATION AND THE PUBLIC SECTOR

When there is great dependence between countries, such as in the EU and in other European countries, it also means that changes in one country will have an impact on the development of the other countries (Blanchard, Leandro, and Zettelmeyer 2021). Larger countries have a greater impact on smaller countries than vice versa, and larger countries in the EU such as the UK (prior to Brexit), Germany and France have as a starting point better options to make national decisions, albeit even large countries are highly dependent on the overall global economic development. Impacts can be felt globally, for example, during the financial crisis, as what started as a bank crash in the US quickly had consequences in a number of other countries and led to large declines in economic activity in a number of other countries as well. Thus, economic growth in a country is also influenced by the international economic development and thereby also the ability to achieve different degrees of macroeconomic balances.

At the same time, the international financial crisis meant that in a number of countries, as a result of the exogenous shock, economic growth became negative and unemployment rose. This despite the fact that even very large economic growth packages were launched, which can to a large extent be characterized as Keynesian-inspired demand management, and this was done even across the more traditional division of welfare states (Vis, Van Kersbergen, and Hylands 2011).

But at the same time, the great interdependence means that it can be difficult for a country to pursue a completely independent national economic and expansive/contractive fiscal policy, as the expansive/contractive fiscal policy will not only lead to increased/decreased activity in the country that implements it, but in all countries with which a high degree of economic cooperation and interaction takes place. Overall, this implies a risk that economic expansive policy is used less than what could be optimal from an economic point of view. This is because if a number of countries all expand their activities in times of economic recessions, this could have a relatively large impact on employment and production. Natural restrictions or international agreements (see Sections 10.3 and 10.4) might imply a reduction of these opportunities.

The international interdependence and influence on each other as countries also means that there are fewer degrees of economic freedom compared to before, so that, for example, monetary policy can only be decided to a more limited extent nationally, and correspondingly that exchange rate policy is greatly influenced by the international economic situation. Countries with floating exchange rates will be able to see that their exchange rates change both upwards and downwards, but at the same time floating exchange rates mean that it is difficult to use them as a separate economic instrument. Large countries may have, as mentioned above, slightly more degrees of economic freedom than other countries, but the international economic crises have shown that crises tend to spread from one country to another.

This can also help in explaining why the so-called Modern Money Theory (MMT) argument that one might finance an expansionary fiscal policy by public sector deficit is not realistic, given the large interdependencies across countries, including that the MMT does not include citizens' expectations of the future in the way that economies function, so that if large deficits occur they will be aware of the risk of rising taxes and duties in the years to come (Palley 2020).

The interdependencies also imply that nation states will have restrictions in the way they can decide to structure their tax system, such as level of taxes, but also rules related to what and how to tax, as already pointed out a long time ago (Genschel 2002). This includes, as an example, the level of corporate tax, which has been reduced over time, but also how the ability to move taxable income around the globe and across countries implies a need for a common framework for the taxation of companies (Valenduc 2018). Tax competition can influence income from and the possible level of corporate tax, but might also influence capital movement, cross-border trade and a number of other issues (Greve 2010; Genschel and Schwarz 2011). Thus, in principle, even if taxation is a national decision issue, it is also an issue of the risk of the possible unintended consequences of taxation on other countries' options. To illustrate this point, see Table 10.1.

As can be witnessed from Table 10.1, in all countries since 2000 there has been a reduction, even though a stronger decline in some countries than in others. In October 2021, 136 OECD countries agreed that multinational companies have to pay a minimum corporate tax rate of 15 per cent in the future[1] on the income generated in a country. How to precisely define the tax base is still an open question.

The interdependencies among countries include that if duties are increased in one country and neighbouring countries have lower duties, the risk is that trade, at least cross-border trade, will move to the countries with lower duties or to the hidden economy. Thereby, decisions on public sector economics are restricted by not only the possible change in behaviour and not just in the context of the influence on the labour supply, but also the situation in other countries.

The free movement of workers within the EU, including the rights of those using that freedom, might also have an impact on national decisions, such as working conditions, but also on the level of social benefits as those fulfilling the rules of the free movement shall, in principle, have access to the same benefits as national citizens under the same conditions.

The EU might also influence types of spending in countries, which is not discussed in detail here, by, for example, demands related to the environment or working conditions.

Table 10.1   *Development in the corporate tax rate in European countries in selected years since 2000*

Year	2000	2005	2010	2015	2020	2021
Austria	34.0	25.0	25.0	25.0	25.0	25.0
Belgium	39.0	33.0	33.0	33.0	25.0	25.0
Czech Republic	31.0	26.0	19.0	19.0	19.0	19.0
Denmark	32.0	28.0	25.0	23.5	22.0	22.0
Estonia	26.0	24.0	21.0	20.0	20.0	20.0
Finland	29.0	26.0	26.0	20.0	20.0	20.0
France	37.8	34.9	34.4	38.0	32.0	28.4
Germany	42.2	26.4	15.8	15.8	15.8	15.8
Greece	40.0	32.0	24.0	29.0	24.0	24.0
Hungary	18.0	16.0	19.0	19.0	9.0	9.0
Ireland	24.0	12.5	12.5	12.5	12.5	12.5
Italy	37.0	33.0	27.5	27.5	24.0	24.0
Latvia	25.0	15.0	15.0	15.0	20.0	20.0
Lithuania	24.0	15.0	15.0	15.0	15.0	15.0
Luxembourg	31.2	22.9	21.8	22.5	18.2	18.2
Netherlands	35.0	31.5	25.5	25.0	25.0	25.0
Poland	30.0	19.0	19.0	19.0	19.0	19.0
Portugal	32.0	25.0	25.0	28.0	30.0	30.0
Slovak Republic	29.0	19.0	19.0	22.0	21.0	21.0
Slovenia	25.0	25.0	20.0	17.0	19.0	19.0
Spain	35.0	35.0	30.0	28.0	25.0	25.0
Sweden	28.0	28.0	26.3	22.0	21.4	20.6
United Kingdom	30.0	30.0	28.0	20.0	19.0	19.0

Source: OECD, Statutory Corporate Income Tax Rates, accessed 2 December, 2021.

10.3   THE EMU IN THE EU

The EU influences national member states' public policy, not only by the rules related to the EMU as described below, but also the attempt to try to coordinate the social and economic policy. Part of this naturally reflects how to cope with the criteria in the EMU, but also that the free movement of workers and an internal market has implications for what the nation state can do, while there is also the option to learn about best practice by comparing with what is happening in other countries (Zeitlin and Vanhercke 2018). Public procurement is also regulated within the EU in order to reduce the risk that nation states favour their own production, and also with the ambition that there is competition among providers of a number of different goods and services.

The development of an economic and monetary union within the EU has a long history (which is not repeated here), and further not all EU member states are part of the union. Those countries that are members of the EMU have to comply with the following issues:

national deficits must not exceed 3% of gross domestic product (GDP), national public debt must remain below 60% of GDP.

as well as:

To comply with this "balanced budget rule", countries must keep their annual structural deficits at 0.5% of GDP or lower. A structural deficit is the general deficit minus the impact of the economic cycle on government spending and revenue (e.g. higher expenditure on unemployment benefits in a recession).

Governments must put in place an automatic correction mechanism triggered by any departure from the balanced budget rule. That means that if the budget balance deviates from the projected line, corrective measures are taken automatically.

Countries may be temporarily exempted from the balanced budget rule in exceptional circumstances, such as a severe economic downturn. Moreover, if a government's public debt is well below the Stability and Growth Pact's reference value (60% of GDP), it may be granted a higher structural deficit of up to 1% of GDP. (Both quotes from https://eur-lex.europa.eu/legal-content/EN/TXT/?uri= LEGISSUM:1403_3, accessed 28 September 2021)

Euro-area countries not complying with the rules might be given a fine of up to 0.5 per cent of GDP. It might further be difficult for countries having a high debt/deficit level to borrow, as was witnessed by the demand on countries to reduce deficits and debts, especially in Southern Europe and Ireland, after the financial crisis, and the consequences hereof (Matsaganis and Leventi 2014; Paulus, Figari, and Sutherland 2016; Skidelsky and Fraccaroli 2017). For a number of countries, compliance with the rules has been more limited.

Most of the countries within the EU use the Euro as currency (19 member states), meaning that they do not have a national currency, and the above-mentioned rules in relation to fiscal deficit and debt imply restrictions on national economic policies (returned to in Section 10.4). Not having a national currency implies that change to the exchange rate is not an available economic instrument, while at the same time implying a pressure that all countries within a monetary and economic union have at least some common rules to avoid, for example, that a large deficit in some countries might have an impact in other countries due to a pressure on the currency. The exchange of the Euro will be more stable with stability in the economy. This also goes for other large currency areas, even if the value depends on the demand and supply hereof, and has a less strong influence hereby, and it will be difficult to speculate against a currency in areas with economic stability.

Whether the indicators should continue in their current form is open for interpretation and discussion, and it is argued that they should be changed given they are not flexible and precise enough, and be more country specific (Blanchard, Leandro, and Zettelmeyer 2021). This is not pursued here, but it reflects the fact that combining the need for overall rules with different national contexts does not imply that it simply can be done.

10.4   DEFICIT, DEBT AND INFLUENCE ON POLICY OPTIONS IN ONE OR MORE NATION STATES

The framework for the general government deficit and debt within EU countries (as mentioned in Section 10.3) provides an indicator that there is and will be a need to look at its size, and not only in countries within the EU. Whether the size of this should be the same as within the EU can be discussed, as the consequences of debt also largely depend on whether the debt is financed by the country's own citizens or is borrowed from other countries. In addition, for large countries, there will generally be less risk that the country's exchange rate may be squeezed. Table 10.2 shows the level of public sector deficits and debts for a few years since 2008.

Table 10.2 is a strong indicator of the large variety in public sector debt, being the highest in Greece in 2020 and the lowest in Estonia. Overall, it is low in Eastern Europe and high in Southern Europe as well as in Belgium, France and the UK. The table also shows the high level of deficit after both the financial crisis (data in 2010) and the COVID-19 crisis (data for 2020). This again is an indicator that the ability to cope with crises and the consequences for the public sector economy in the future can be highly influenced by the level before the onset of exogenous shocks on an economy. Those with high levels of debts will be in a more precarious position to cope with the shock. At the same time, using the public sector to help manage economic development is important, and also that the measurement of debt does not necessarily include all important information, such as on the value of public investment in infrastructure.

Still, the reason why there is a need to look at the size of government deficits and government debt is because countries with large deficits and high debt in relation to the country's economy will have the risk of having to pay a higher interest rate on loans than countries with low debt. Thus, a country risks that higher interest payments mean that it may be more difficult to finance other public activities, and thus risks ending up in a downward spiral where increasing interest payments lead to pressure on other public sector expenditure.

Table 10.2   Development in yearly public sector deficit and debt as % of GDP in selected years since 2000

Time	Yearly deficit as proportion of GDP						Debt as proportion of GDP in selected years					
	2000	2005	2010	2015	2019	2020	2000	2005	2010	2015	2019	2020
EU27	-1.2	-2.3	-6.0	-1.9	-0.5	-6.9	66.3	67.1	80.4	84.7	77.2	90.1
Belgium	-0.1	-2.7	-4.1	-2.4	-1.9	-9.1	109.6	95.1	100.3	105.2	97.7	112.8
Bulgaria	0.1	1.6	-3.7	-1.9	2.1	-4.0	70.7	26.6	15.3	25.9	20.0	24.7
Czechia	-3.6	-3.0	-4.2	-0.6	0.3	-5.6	17.0	27.7	37.1	39.7	30.0	37.7
Denmark	1.9	5.0	-2.7	-1.2	4.1	-0.2	52.4	37.4	42.6	39.8	33.6	42.1
Germany	-1.6	-3.3	-4.4	1.0	1.5	-4.3	59.3	67.5	82.0	72.0	58.9	68.7
Estonia	-0.1	1.1	0.2	0.1	0.1	-5.6	5.1	4.7	6.7	10.1	8.6	19.0
Ireland	4.9	1.6	-32.1	-2.0	0.5	-4.9	36.4	26.1	86.2	76.7	57.2	58.4
Greece	-4.1	-6.2	-11.3	-5.9	1.1	-10.1	104.9	107.4	147.5	176.7	180.7	206.3
Spain	-1.2	1.2	-9.5	-5.2	-2.9	-11.0	57.8	42.4	60.5	99.3	95.5	120.0
France	-1.3	-3.4	-6.9	-3.6	-3.1	-9.1	58.9	67.4	85.3	95.6	97.5	115.0
Croatia	-3.0	-3.5	-6.4	-3.4	0.3	-7.4	35.4	40.9	57.3	83.3	71.1	87.3
Italy	-2.4	-4.1	-4.2	-2.6	-1.5	-9.6	109.0	106.6	119.2	135.3	134.3	155.6
Cyprus	-2.2	-2.2	-4.7	-0.9	1.3	-5.7	55.7	63.4	56.4	107.2	91.1	115.3
Latvia	-2.7	-0.5	-8.6	-1.4	-0.6	-4.5	12.1	11.9	47.7	37.1	36.7	43.2
Lithuania	-3.2	-0.3	-6.9	-0.3	0.5	-7.2	23.5	17.6	36.2	42.5	35.9	46.6
Luxembourg	5.5	-0.2	-0.3	1.3	2.3	-3.5	7.5	8.0	19.1	21.1	22.3	24.8
Hungary	-3.0	-7.8	-4.4	-2.0	-2.1	-8.0	55.7	60.5	80.0	75.7	65.5	80.1
Malta	-5.5	-2.8	-2.3	-0.8	0.5	-9.7	60.7	69.9	65.5	56.3	40.7	53.4
Netherlands	1.2	-0.4	-5.3	-2.1	1.7	-4.2	52.1	49.8	59.2	64.6	48.5	54.3

Time	Yearly deficit as proportion of GDP						Debt as proportion of GDP in selected years					
	2000	2005	2010	2015	2019	2020	2000	2005	2010	2015	2019	2020
Austria	-2.4	-2.5	-4.4	-1.0	0.6	-8.3	66.1	68.6	82.7	84.9	70.6	83.2
Poland	-4.0	-3.9	-7.4	-2.6	-0.7	-7.1	36.4	46.6	53.5	51.3	45.6	57.4
Portugal	-3.2	-6.1	-11.4	-4.4	0.1	-5.8	54.2	72.2	100.2	131.2	116.6	135.2
Romania	-4.6	-0.8	-6.9	-0.6	-4.4	-9.4	22.5	15.9	29.6	37.8	35.3	47.4
Slovenia	-3.6	-1.3	-5.6	-2.8	0.4	-7.7	25.9	26.4	38.3	82.6	65.6	79.8
Slovakia	-12.6	-2.9	-7.5	-2.7	-1.3	-5.5	50.5	34.7	40.8	51.8	48.1	59.7
Finland	6.9	2.7	-2.5	-2.4	-0.9	-5.5	42.5	39.9	46.9	63.6	59.5	69.5
Sweden	3.1	1.8	-0.1	0.0	0.6	-2.8	50.3	48.7	38.1	43.7	34.9	39.7
UK	1.35	-3.11	-9.23	-4.54	-2.33	-12.3	49.3	52.1	89.4	112.7	117.2	144.1

Source: Eurostat ([GOV_10DD_EDPT1__custom_1634743]) and for the UK: https://data.oecd.org/gga/general-government-deficit.htm#indicator-chart, accessed 24 November 2021.

It also means that countries with a high debt level if there is a crisis will have more difficulty in using intervention in the economy with change in either expenditures and/or taxes and duties as new debt can be very expensive (naturally depending on the ongoing interest rate in the international money market). This was seen during the financial crisis and also during the COVID-19 crisis, when it was easier to expand the public sector for those countries with a low level of debt compared to other countries.

It also implies that countries with a high level of deficit, except in crisis situations, will need to try to reduce the level hereof. This can, theoretically, be done by increasing the level of taxes and duties and/or by reducing public spending. The consequences of this will depend on the more precise composition and weighting of different instruments (see more in Chapters 5 and 6).

It is not discussed here whether, for example, there were countries that have benefited from other countries' government deficits (e.g. through interest payments), or ability to sell its goods and services, and furthermore how much debt forgiveness was necessary to ensure a continued stable economic development in Europe. The key is that countries with limited debt are relatively better able to cope with exogenous shocks, including being able to change through both the automatic stabilizers and an active fiscal policy (either changes in taxes and duties or public spending).

This reflects another problem in the regulation of the public sector economy that changes in one country can affect the development of another country. This applies to both expansion and contraction in the public sector economy in that, through its influence also on the private sector's demand for goods and services, it affects not only domestic production, but also other countries' producers. Therefore, if many producers at the same time reduce or increase their economic activity, this can amplify or diminish the overall economic effects in many countries at once. This also illustrates why economic crises can spread quickly from one country to many others.

It will therefore also be a constant challenge for countries to balance the need for changes in the public sector's short-term economic impact on societal development with long-term opportunities. For example, it is possible that an expansive fiscal policy is needed here and now, but if it increases the deficit significantly and there is a new exogenous crisis that affects the public sector, then it may be difficult to do as desired. This also indicates the need to ensure that decisions to ensure a good public sector economy are made in good times, which enable a country to act in less good times in order to keep the economy functioning as best as possible when there is both high and low economic activity.

10.5   TAX COMPETITION[2]

The financing of welfare states is influenced by a number of issues. Globalization, as mentioned above, is one issue. As a result of globalization, a possible risk is that large companies will not pay taxes (by moving to tax havens and/or by looking for tax holes) on their activities, and thus increasing the pressure on the welfare state (Cournède, Fournier, and Hoeller 2018). More widely, this can be reflected at the international level by the ambition to ensure a common framework for paying taxes within the EU, the so-called Common-Consolidated-Corporate-Tax-Base (CCCTB)[3] (see also Valenduc 2018), the aim being to ensure a more consistent taxing of the international companies within the EU. There is also ongoing work among 135 countries to avoid what is labelled Base Erosion and Profit Shifting (BEPS) among countries, which is estimated to cause a loss of corporate tax revenue of between 4 per cent and 10 per cent of GDP.[4] This also includes debates on how to tax companies based upon location (see also Section 10.2 on the agreement on a minimum tax rate in October 2021). A tax on the turnover of a company's activities, and how to use transfer-pricing rules, can be new ways of ensuring a stable revenue (Keen and Slemrod 2021). Transfer-pricing rules are difficult, and an important issue in financing the public sector is how to make the rules fair while reducing the risk that companies make sure that their "surplus" is mainly in either tax havens or at least countries with the lowest corporate tax rates.

Reduced public sector income from taxation might also be due to tax avoidance, including using transfer prices as a way of paying a lower amount of money than in principle should be the case. Thus, further trying to reduce direct tax avoidance as well as to increase tax compliance can be important as a way of ensuring the necessary financing for the public sector in all countries in the years to come (Manning 2015).

In some countries there is the risk that the difference in taxation between the employed and self-employed implies a risk of tax arbitrage, and thereby lower tax revenue. This is especially the case where part of the overall financing is due to social security contributions paid by the employer for the employed, given there is not the same responsibility to do that for the self-employed (Milanez and Bratta 2019). Thus, due to new technology and ways of working, the increase in the number of solo-self-employed including more work related to the development of platforms is influencing not only job insecurity, but also state insecurity.

Besides pressures related to technology and globalization, there is also the issue that some believe in what has been labelled trickle-down economics or Reaganomics (Chomsky 2007), that is, even if the rich get richer due to tax cuts, then this will also imply better living standards for those with low incomes. Lowering taxes has been argued also to imply a higher labour supply, which should then make it possible to have a higher level of production (see also the discussions hereabout in Chapter 6).

It seems, however, that it has not been possible to document such effects, given that "no study to date has been able to show convincing evidence in the short or medium run of large real economic activity responses of upper earners to tax rates" (Piketty and Stantcheva 2014, 231). It has also been shown that in-work benefits, which should also make work more attractive, have different impacts across countries, so that one might not be sure that increasing incentives will, in fact, increase the labour supply (Vandelannoote and Verbist 2020). Lastly, there is increasing knowledge that taxation can be done in a number of ways, and that there is, in fact, a case for progressive tax (Diamond and Saez 2011).

10.6   CONCLUSIONS

A country works with, and is dependent on, the economic development of other countries. This also affects the development of the country's public sector, and places restrictions on, for example, how large a public finance deficit and how much public debt a country can have if it is to have sufficient economic freedom to act even in situations of change in the overall regional or global economic development.

In addition (as pointed out in Chapter 7 and Section 10.5), the possibility for countries to collect taxes and duties is challenged by the internationalization of economies, while there is a risk that the tax base is eroded, especially as a result of large multinational companies, but also the platform economy. The implication is that the options to finance public sector activity in one direction or another is more difficult.

It thus requires that financial decisions not only take into account the short term, but also ensure that there will be room and the opportunity to cope with challenges that appear suddenly, that is, long-term considerations are also important.

NOTES

1.   https://www.oecd.org/tax/international-community-strikes-a-ground-breaking -tax-deal-for-the-digital-age.htm, accessed 12 December 2021.
2.   This section comes mainly from Section 6.4 in Greve (2022).
3.   See https://ec.europa.eu/taxation_customs/business/company-tax/common-con solidated-corporate-tax-base-ccctb_en, accessed 25 January 2021.
4.   See https://www.oecd.org/tax/beps/, accessed 25 January 2021.

REFERENCES

Blanchard, Olivier, Alvaro Leandro, and Jeromin Zettelmeyer. 2021. "Redesigning EU Fiscal Rules: From Rules to Standards." *Economic Policy* 21: 1.

Chomsky, Aviva. 2007. *"They Take Our Jobs!": And 20 Other Myths about Immigration.* Boston: Beacon Press.

Cournède, Boris, Jean-Marc Fournier, and Peter Hoeller. 2018. "Public Finance Structure and Inclusive Growth," no. 25. https://doi.org/10.1787/e99683b5-en.

Diamond, Peter, and Emmanuel Saez. 2011. "The Case for a Progressive Tax: From Basic Research to Policy Recommendations." *Journal of Economic Perspectives* 25 (4): 165–90.

Genschel, Philipp. 2002. "Globalization, Tax Competition, and the Welfare State." *Politics & Society* 30 (2): 245–75.

Genschel, Philipp, and Peter Schwarz. 2011. "Tax Competition: A Literature Review." *Socio-Economic Review* 9 (2): 339–70.

Greve, B. 2010. "Taxation, Equality and Social Cohesion European Experiences." In *Challenges of Social Cohesion in Times of Crisis: Euro-Latin American Dialogue*, edited by E. Zupi and M. Estruch Puertas, 307–32. Madrid: FIIAPP.

Greve, B. 2022. *Rethinking the Welfare State.* Cheltenham, UK and Northampton, MA, USA: Edward Elgar Publishing.

Keen, Michael, and Joel Slemrod. 2021. *Rebellion, Rascals, and Revenue. Tax Follies and Wisdon through the Ages.* Princeton, NJ: Princeton University Press.

Manning, Alan. 2015. "Top Rate of Income Tax." London: Centre for Economic Performance.

Matsaganis, Manos, and Chrysa Leventi. 2014. "The Distributional Impact of Austerity and the Recession in Southern Europe." *South European Society & Politics* 19 (3): 393–412. http://10.0.4.56/13608746.2014.947700.

Milanez, Anna, and Barbara Bratta. 2019. "Taxation and the Future of Work: How Tax Systems Influence Choice of Employment Form." OECD Taxation Working Papers. Paris: OECD. https://doi.org/10.1787/20f7164a-en.

Palley, Thomas. 2020. "What's Wrong with Modern Money Theory: Macro and Political Economic Restraints on Deficit-Financed Fiscal Policy." *Review of Keynesian Economics* 8 (4): 472–93.

Paulus, Alari, Francesco Figari, and Holly Sutherland. 2016. "The Design of Fiscal Consolidation Measures in the European Union: Distributional Effects and Implications for Macro-Economic Recovery." *Oxford Economic Papers*, 1–23. https://doi.org/10.1093/oep/afw054.

Piketty, T., and S. Stantcheva. 2014. "Optimal Taxation of Labor Income. A Tale of Three Elasticities." *American Economic Journal: Economic Policy* 6 (1): 230–71.

Skidelsky, Robert, and Nicoló Fraccaroli (eds). 2017. *Austerity vs Stimulus: The Political Future of Economic Recovery.* Cham: Palgrave Macmillan. https://doi.org/10.1007/978-3-319-50439-1.

Valenduc, Christian. 2018. "Corporate Income Tax in the EU, the Common Consolidated Corporate Tax Base (CCCTB) and Beyond: Is It the Right Way to Go?" *ETUI Research Paper – Working Paper*.

Vandelannoote, Dieter, and Gerlinde Verbist. 2020. "The Impact of In-Work Benefits on Work Incentives and Poverty in Four European Countries." *Journal of European Social Policy*, 0958928719891314.

Vis, Barbara, Kees Van Kersbergen, and Tom Hylands. 2011. "To What Extent Did the Financial Crisis Intensify the Pressure to Reform the Welfare State?" *Social Policy & Administration* 45 (4): 338–53.

Zeitlin, Jonathan, and Bart Vanhercke. 2018. "Socializing the European Semester: EU Social and Economic Policy Co-ordination in Crisis and Beyond." *Journal of European Public Policy* 25 (2): 149–74.

11. A social investment perspective on public sector spending

11.1 INTRODUCTION

There is ongoing discussion of the possible influence of the public sector on the overall economic impact, especially when focusing on issues outside purely public goods, as well as on broader societal development. Further, there is a need to investigate public sector economics not only in the short run, but also what might work and influence the development in the longer-term perspective. This is part of the debate as to whether the public sector is a burden for societies or part of the solution for a better society. Thus, in Section 11.2, the chapter starts by presenting the idea of social investment, but also the possible difficulties in measuring it, and possible ethical challenges of using a social investment perspective in public sector economics. This is followed in Section 11.3 with examples of types of social investment policies in the field of social policy, and Section 11.4 presents and discusses the role of, and possible influence on, research and industrial development.

In Section 11.5, the chapter looks into the possible dynamic impact of different types of public sector spending, as well as the discussion on what happens to the labour supply as a consequence of changes in the income tax system. It also discusses whether, even if knowing that there might be a positive impact on certain types of spending, one is able to measure the size and impact of a marginal change in spending in one area. This could, for example, be one extra hour of teaching or fewer children in a class. Section 11.6 then sums up the chapter.

11.2 THE SOCIAL INVESTMENT PERSPECTIVE

When and how the idea of a social investment perspective of the role of the state was first presented can be discussed. It might be argued that Giddens's third way approach was an element hereof (Giddens 2008), and later also the EU entered into debates on how to understand the role of the state not as just expenditures, but also as investments in the future. This included: "Progress on putting an increased focus on social investment in their social policies such as (child)care, education, training, active labour market policies, housing support, rehabilitation and health services" (https://eur-lex.europa.eu/legal-content/EN/ TXT/PDF/?uri=CELEX:52013DC0083&from=EN, p. 22).

The EU has also highlighted social investment as:

> Ensuring that social protection systems respond to people's needs at critical moments throughout their lives. More needs to be done to reduce the risk of social breakdown and so avoid higher social spending in the future.
>
> Simplified and better targeted social policies, to provide adequate and sustainable social protection systems. Some countries have better social outcomes than others despite having similar or lower budgets, demonstrating that there is room for more efficient social policy spending.
>
> Upgrading active inclusion strategies in the Member States. Affordable quality childcare and education, prevention of early school leaving, training and job-search assistance, housing support and accessible health care are all policy areas with a strong social investment dimension. (http://europa.eu/rapid/press-release_IP-13 -125_en.htm)

The social investment approach thus has as a focus that at least part of the public sector activities should bring about better overall societal development. This includes, for example, how to combine work and family life. Investment in education can also help to ensure higher competitiveness, implying that social policy is supporting economic growth and job creation.

A social investment policy has as central focus "that both invest in human capital development (early childhood education and care, education and life-long training) and that help to make efficient use of human capital …, while fostering greater social inclusion" (Morel, Palier, and Palme 2012, 2).

The possible policies and instruments in a social investment policy could include: human capital investment policies to increase competitiveness and job creation; development of social services and policies to support the labour market; early childhood education and care; higher education and life-long training; Active Labour Market Policies (ALMPs); policies to support women's employment; flexi-security (Morel, Palier, and Palme 2012).

Still, it has been argued that it is not enough to have a specific type of policy to label it social investment. As argued, "the agenda of the social investment state includes active labour market policy, not in the sense of 'workfare', i.e., bullying unemployed people to take any job available, but in providing train-ing and help with job search, perhaps with removal costs" (Crouch 2013, 89). However, to measure the impact of different types of ALMP might be more difficult.

Therefore also, if the understanding of social investment policies includes an interpretation of the qualitative aspect of the investment, this will make it even more difficult to measure the impact hereof. Whether countries follow a social investment approach further depends on what type of expenditures are seen as social investment policies, including whether all the spending in an area can be considered as such or whether only to a more limited extent. Even day-care for children, often seen as social investment, can have a number of different elements that can influence the understanding and measurements of the impact hereof.

Naturally, there is the risk that the different perspectives can be used by pressure groups to ensure more spending in their area (Leoni 2016; Midgley, Dahl, and Wright 2017), and thereby one will need also to look into the data and evidence that a specific type of spending has a specific societal impact on the development. Still, social investment can be a type of spending which can have a number of side-effects. This can also help in explaining that even if economic analysis suggests a positive societal outcome of an investment, there might not be support from voters for it, as they prefer either spending or investment in other areas of societal development, especially when investments might imply a cutback in other types of social spending (Neimanns, Busemeyer, and Garritzmann 2018). It is the case, for example, that the risk of automation of jobs for individuals is negatively related to the support for social investments (Busemeyer and Sahm 2021).

There are a number of methodological issues related to the understanding of the impact of social investment, as described earlier in the book in relation to cost-benefit and cost-effectiveness analysis. These include:

- The time-period to consider, including what discount factor to use.
- The type of social investment and risk to include in the calculation.
- Which social impact to include in the analysis.
- To measure the quality of a specific change in services – especially if it is to be monetized (see also 11.5).
- What the investment is, and what the compensatory expenditures are.
- The ability to finance investment even if it implies a surplus in the future.

Therefore, the analysis of social investment needs to be done by clearly informing about what is and is not included in the analysis and criteria. This also includes what spending is normal "expenditure" and which can be considered investment. This has also been an issue when trying to analyse whether there has been increased spending on social investment.

Furthermore, there have been difficulties in arguing what type of welfare spending is social investment and what is not. For example, ALMP is seen as social investment, but if it has been there for a long time, such as in the Nordic welfare states in Europe, one might question whether this has been a turn towards social investment. The distinction between consumption and investment expenditures is thereby blurred (Beramendi et al. 2015; Kuitto 2016). The consumption category typically includes policy measures that help people to cope with loss of income, whether due to old age, family responsibilities or illness, and are often labelled mainly old social risks and with a strong focus on income transfers. The investment category includes expenditures that, like ALMP, help people and enhance their employability. However, the boundaries between consumption and investment are often blurred, and the same holds true for boundaries between different policy areas. For instance, day-care for children and early pre-school is on the border between education and family policies, while at the same time enabling both parents to be on the labour market. Similarly, it is difficult to define whether different interventions prevent or repair damage, including what has been known for a long time in social policy that prevention can be best (Berghman, Debels, and Van Hoyweghen 2019). Social investment might thus at the same time be a new argument for public sector intervention, while at the same time some of the arguments overlap with the issues related to how to cope with a number of the market failures.

It has also been pointed out that there is a risk of a stronger focus on social investment causing a bias towards the interests of the middle classes (e.g. education, childcare, life-long learning) at the expense of the lower classes (Cantillon 2011). There is also an argument of the risk of crowding out the social policies related to redistribution and initiatives mainly for the lower-income groups (Nolan 2013). Still, others point out that some policies might reduce income inequality, whereas other policies do not, so that parental leave reduces economic inequality, but other types of family policy do not. Also, there is no clear information as to how education and ALMP influence inequality, and that it might even vary across countries (Sakamoto 2021). This implies that empirical analysis is needed in each country to also consider the national context. The variation in outcome might also help in explaining that, among different groups of citizens, there can be variation in their support for initiatives having a social investment perspective (Bledow and Busemeyer 2020).

Furthermore, if decisions are based only upon economic calculations, including, for example, labour market participation, then there can be an ethical issue as this will favour those who are youngest and have the longest time perspective to be productive, which would then disfavour the elderly with their possible need for care. This means that one needs to be aware of how to calculate the value of protecting the elderly (Parolin and Van Lancker 2021). Thereby, the analysis of social investment might need not only to consider the result of an economic analysis, but also to take a closer look at the criteria that have been used in the calculations. There will also be a need in a number of areas to assess how the quality of a service is to be calculated, and how requirements and expectations for quality can be included in calculations and assessments of which efforts are to be promoted as much as possible. Similarly, it can be methodically difficult to determine which "needs" require an effort from the welfare state. Needs are thus not necessarily something that can be easily calculated and assessed, just as there can be difficulties in comparing across a number of welfare areas. How to include the impact on well-being in the assessment of social investment policies can also be a challenge, despite the fact that we know that there is a positive impact (Kolev and Tassot 2016). This also increases the need for transparency and knowledge of how different calculations have been made when prioritizing. For a discussion on how to measure and what needs to be included, see the debate in these articles: Parolin and Van Lancker (2021); Hemerijck and Plavgo (2021); Plavgo and Hemerijck (2020). The data and choice hereof can also be an issue, for an example of the collection of data, see Ronchi (2016, 2018).

The generational issue is also present in the analysis of environmental issues where there might be long-term gain, which can be different gains between the young and the elderly.

11.3   EXAMPLES OF SOCIAL INVESTMENT

A number of examples can be given of what is meant by social investment. Typically, in continuation of the discussion in the previous section, emphasis is placed on expenses that have a number of effects on what opportunities the individual/family can and does have as a result of the investment. It therefore includes how to increase capabilities, in Sen's understanding hereof (Sen 2006, 2008), in the individual household.

It can be about increasing the possibility of finding employment, to ensure that citizens have sufficient social and human capital to be able to do better in getting or keeping their job. It is thus tasks from areas such as the ALMP, but also childcare as well as education that can be characterized as social investments. The same applies to the extent that, for example, the elderly, through various forms of support, become better able to manage on their own, can be characterized as social investments. An issue related to social investment for the elderly is whether this can be measured, and also whether stakeholders are aware hereof (Greve 2018).

Thus, it can also be difficult for economic analysis to argue for choosing one type of social investment over another because, in addition to the previously mentioned ethical aspects playing a role, so do elements such as time horizon, needs and quality of services. On the other hand, economic analysis can to a much greater extent compare and evaluate different efforts against the same problems, and here, based on, for example, cost-benefit or cost-effectiveness analysis, it can argue for the choice of one intervention compared with a number of other types of interventions.

Figure 11.1 shows the development in spending since 2000 on different types of family policies for the EU-25 (data incomplete for Bulgaria and Croatia).

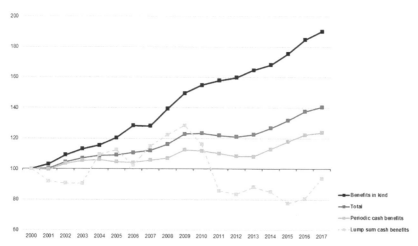

Source: https://ec.europa.eu/eurostat/statistics-explained/index.php?title=Social_protection _statistics_-_family_and_children_benefits, accessed 20 September 2021.

Figure 11.1   *Developments for expenditure on family/children benefits at constant prices by type of disbursement, EU-27, 2000–17*

As can be witnessed from Figure 11.1, there has been a strong increase in spending on benefits in-kind, which is mainly day-care for children. This is an indicator that since the millennium, social investment with regard to childcare has been an increased priority in most European countries, and the expenditure on day-care for children has more than doubled since 2000. Thus, this is a clear indicator of a shift towards a social investment perspective, given that available day-care facilities for children also increase the likelihood that both men and women will be able to take jobs at the labour market, thereby supporting families' choice of how to combine work and family life.

It is possible to examine whether there has been a diversion towards more social investment by using either national data for the country one would like to investigate or by comparative analysis of data from Eurostat or the OECD. It is important to describe why the areas have been selected and the time horizon over which the analysis is carried out. For example, there may be a risk, as indicated earlier in the chapter in relation to ALMPs, that some countries already have high expenditure in this area, but also that expenditure on this type of investment may fluctuate with the degree of unemployment. The long-term value of the investment can be difficult to measure because there can be a number of other factors that influence the development.

It may be, for example, that even if rehabilitation efforts are carried out for the elderly (Greve 2016), there may be uncertainty as to whether there will be new diseases, which will mean that the efforts will not have the necessary effect. Therefore, there will be a need for clarity and awareness that effects can change over time and be influenced by other external influences. This is also the case when looking into how formal care can have an impact on the health of carers (who are, typically, daughters). One study showed that it had an impact on the health of daughters in the short run, but not in the long run (Abrahamsen and Grøtting 2019), while at the same time it might influence labour market participation.

Knowing that income and at risk of poverty might have an impact on children's long-term behaviour as well as health could imply that using an unconditional benefit could be beneficial. This is confirmed in an American study, which also refers to other studies indicating the same (Akee et al. 2018).

11.4   RESEARCH AND STRUCTURAL POLICY

Public spending can have both short-term and long-term effects on the development of society. Infrastructure costs have very long-term effects, given that, for example, bridges have a very long physical durability. But the same applies to investments in research and development, which can greatly contribute to companies having better opportunities to develop new products. Even Apple's development, for example, has largely been linked to investment and intervention by the US government (Mazzucato 2013).

Public research and development, including education, can thus be important for the emergence of sufficient new ideas for the development of production and new products, as well as having the necessary social and human capital that is important for the overall economic development.

It also means that since it can be difficult to predict whether basic research, in particular, will yield results, there will be projects that fail. The balance for the public sector economy will thus be, on the one hand, to have a sufficient willingness to take risks and, on the other hand, be prepared to spend money on creating new ideas, products and ways that can support societal development, including private company opportunities. Creating common knowledge by supporting research might also imply more public goods in the sense that if it is open knowledge then one person's use of the knowledge does not, at least at the outset, reduce another person's use of the good.

This is also an issue related to research, for example, within medicine. Given research is very expensive to do including the demand for trials and tests, companies might only get their money back if they have a monopoly position (patents) lasting for a number of years – often ten years. Thereby private research, which also might fail, will not necessarily be available for all, and even be an example that a monopoly might be accepted for a limited time.

Education is a key area for the public sector in many countries. This is partly due to the fact that education contributes to the development of human capital, but also because it will be an area which, if left to the market, will mean that fewer people will receive an education than would otherwise be the case, the merit-good argument. This is because preferences are different, but also because there is a difference in risk behaviour and willingness to take a risk. Therefore, if there is a user fee, some will refrain from taking an education. Thus the risk is that a market solution will imply too little education, but naturally also a risk that government financing will imply too much (government failure).

In principle, the economic logic behind user charges is that they should make the individual consider the importance of the good in question (in this case, education) in relation to others. But here the risk is that society's human capital becomes too limited, and thus that the economic development becomes less strong than it would otherwise be.

Therefore, education, at least until higher education, is typically free in most countries, as education provides human capital, but it can also contribute to the individual being able to make more informed choices, and greater equality in education also contributes to a greater degree of economic equality.

However, it can also be difficult here to measure the impact, for example, of more and/or better qualified teachers. One study seems to indicate that better qualified teachers imply that more get a good education and higher income later in life (Chetty, Friedman, and Rockoff 2014). One question is whether teachers' ability to improve test-scores is a good proxy for quality, and whether it is the same in all countries. Still, there is no disagreement that good education can be an important instrument in order to improve societies' abilities to cope with changes, such as new technology.

Financing development in infrastructure (whether it is roads, ports, airports, bridges or IT) can have an impact on how efficiently companies can produce and sell their goods and services. The extent to which the government makes these facilities available either free of charge or for a limited fee could affect a country's competitiveness. Thus, in this way, there are also derived effects of investing in infrastructure. Similarly, public transport can also contribute to more people being able to take care of their work and/or social relations and thus has secondary societal economic consequences.

In relation to payment for this, once infrastructure investments have been made, the money has been used, and thus the payment for using the infrastructure from an economic point of view must correspond only to the marginal costs of use. This does not change the fact that when investing in infrastructure as a whole, consideration must be given to which ones give the greatest possible return on investment. Travel and public transport, for example, can save travel time, but the impact on the environment could also be included in such calculations.

11.5   DO WE KNOW THE IMPACT OF CHANGES INCLUDING ON BEHAVIOUR?

A key problem for the management of, and decision making on, public spending, including for social investment, is that although we know that something can be effective and important for the development of society, and also that it can have a number of long-term effects, it is not a given that we know quality level of a service. Nor is it given that we know whether a marginal improvement in the effort within an area provides so much extra value that it may make sense to use the scarce public resources on it. Further, whether as a consequence of change it will influence behaviour. This, in relation to labour supply, is discussed in Chapter 5.

Theoretically, the marginal extra cost of producing a unit more (or improving the quality of performance) should match the extra benefit that comes from incurring this cost. It is theoretically no different than when private companies have to decide whether they are hiring an extra person which is dependent on increased production so that it can financially be reasonable to be hiring one more person. The problem for the public sector is that for part of the production of public services, it can be difficult to assess its quality.

This does not change the fact that there may be a desire to know what it means if a decision is made in a number of service areas. For example, the consequences of hiring more employees may be to change the quality and/or scope of the service that can be provided within the area in question, but may also be related to a desire for better working conditions for employees, for example. More employees do not even always have to mean better service if the increase is because there are more users, for example, as a result of changes in the demographics in a society.

Quality, especially, can be difficult to measure, particularly in areas such as care and nursing, but also in education, as quality here is also influenced by the personal relationships between employees and users. It can therefore also be a question not only about the number of employees, but also what competencies they have and how the management works within an area. The principal–agent issue can thus also have implications for, and consequences on, changes to spending in different areas, including implying a risk that what works efficiently in some places does not necessarily work in all places.

A measurement issue also arises with regard to possible influence on behaviour. When there are changes in public spending, it can also lead to changes in behaviour, often referred to as a dynamic effect. As a consequence, it is possible that there may have been a larger or smaller supply of labour, but also more or fewer people who, for example, carry out other activities. This means that when the effects of public expenditure are to be assessed, in relation to the net expenditure in the event of changes, account must be taken of:

(a)   The directly decided cost of the activity
(b)   The increase in public revenues due to higher activity (taxes and duties)
(c)   Changes in behaviour that have an impact on public budgets.

In relation to the latter, these behavioural changes can be difficult to predict and also measure, just as there may be effects in the short term, but also some that will have an impact in the longer term.

Where the purchase of more goods and services by the public sector can directly influence demand, increasing the level of education or increasing the quality of childcare, for example, can take many years before effects can be assumed. In both the latter cases, it can also be difficult to assess marginal effects.

Investments in infrastructure (roads, ports, IT, for example) can have both short- and long-term effects where it is necessary to assess whether and how they can influence societal activity.

Effects can also be opposite. On the one hand, better roads can, for example, mean that people can get to their destination faster and thus save time, but also, on the other hand, that more CO_2 is used and emitted as a result. This is an illustration that in addition to the effect on, for example, labour supply, there may also be other derived consequences of public sector investment. At the same time, investment can affect the competitiveness of business and thus the possibility of, for example, reducing unemployment in a country.

Overall, this means that when assessments of public investments are to be made, there will be a number of elements that must be calculated and weighed together, for example, through a cost-benefit analysis (see more in Chapter 7). There are not always good enough data for this as it can be difficult to measure and set a monetary price of investments, such as being able to reduce travel time to work, to have cleaner air, and so on. The monetization of quality of care for the elderly is also difficult and might easily include normative viewpoints of what the good life is.

Therefore, in economic analysis, it may be necessary to separate calculations of what can be done, based on reliable data, figures and money, from a description of a number of possible good effects of spending money on, for example, better care and nursing. Similarly, the fact is that there may be ethical considerations in whether better health can best "pay off" for young people, who have many years left in the labour market, must mean that these groups have to be given priority over service to older people, including whether people who, for example, have retired from the better living conditions of the labour market should not be included in the assessment of how a society develops.

Generational considerations and how they should be priced are similarly difficult, and central here is that it needs to be clear on what terms the calculations have been made. Of greater significance to how the overall result looks is the discount factor used.

11.6   CONCLUSIONS

The idea of social investment challenges the notion that public spending is a burden only for the overall development of society, but that spending to a large extent supports the development of society overall as well as possibilities for the private sector. This may be in the form of higher economic growth, including greater labour supply, but also in the form of a better environment and quality in the provision of a number of essential welfare services. Social investment can, in some fields, be argued to be based upon a merit-good argument, such as in education, that is, that without public sector intervention there will be too little spending in the area.

At the same time, however, there are difficulties in assessing the consequences of minor changes and marginal adjustments, for example, if there is money and the desire for more staff to provide welfare services. Here, there may be a need for both economic analyses, as far as technically possible, and political decisions on how to balance spending between different welfare areas.

The chapter provides examples of a number of social investments, such as childcare and education, but at the same time it points out that there may be a risk that, if economic outcome is used alone as a criterion, it can lead to ethical issues in choices between different spending options. This also means that there will and can be political priorities related to the choices between different areas. At the same time, when relating decisions to a single area, economic analyses will largely be useful for assessing the extent to which there are credible data that inform as fully as possible what can be achieved for the extra cost.

REFERENCES

Abrahamsen, Signe A., and Maja Weemes Grøtting. 2019. *Formal Care of the Elderly and Health Outcomes among Adult Daughters*. Department of Economics, University of Bergen.

Akee, Randall, William Copeland, E. Jane Costello, and Emilia Simeonova. 2018. "How Does Household Income Affect Child Personality Traits and Behaviors?" *American Economic Review* 108 (3): 775–827.

Beramendi, Pablo, Silja Häusermann, Herbert Kitschelt, and Hanspeter Kriesi. 2015. *The Politics of Advanced Capitalism.* Cambridge: Cambridge University Press.

Berghman, J., A. Debels, and I. Van Hoyweghen. 2019. "Prevention: The Cases of Social Security and Healthcare." In *Routledge Handbook of the Welfare State*, edited by B. Greve, 2nd edn, 46–57. Oxon: Routledge.

Bledow, Nona, and Marius R. Busemeyer. 2020. "Lukewarm or Enthusiastic Supporters? Exploring Union Member Attitudes towards Social Investment and Compensatory Policy." *Journal of European Social Policy*, 0958928720974182.

Busemeyer, Marius R., and Alexander H.J. Sahm. 2021. "Social Investment, Redistribution or Basic Income? Exploring the Association between Automation Risk and Welfare State Attitudes in Europe." *Journal of Social Policy*, 1–20. doi:10 .1017/S0047279421000519.

Cantillon, Bea. 2011. "The Paradox of the Social Investment State: Growth, Employment and Poverty in the Lisbon Era." *Journal of European Social Policy* 21 (5): 432–49.

Chetty, Raj, John N. Friedman, and Jonah E. Rockoff. 2014. "Measuring the Impacts of Teachers II: Teacher Value-Added and Student Outcomes in Adulthood." *American Economic Review* 104 (9): 2633–79.

Crouch, Colin. 2013. *Making Capitalism Fit for Society.* Cambridge: Polity Press.

Giddens, Anthony. 2008. *The Third Way.* Cambridge: Polity Press.

Greve, B. (ed.) 2016. *Long-Term Care for the Elderly in Europe: Development and Prospects.* 1st edn. Oxon: Routledge. https://doi.org/10.4324/9781315592947.

Greve, B. 2018. "Do Stakeholders in Denmark Know about Social Investment within Long-Term Care?" *Journal of International and Comparative Social Policy.* https:// doi.org/10.1080/21699763.2018.1465447.

Hemerijck, Anton, and Ilze Plavgo. 2021. "Measuring Returns on Social Investment beyond Here-and-Now Redistribution: A Commentary on Parolin and Van Lancker's Response Article." *Journal of European Social Policy* 31 (3): 309–20.

Kolev, Alexandre, and Caroline Tassot. 2016. "Can Investments in Social Protection Contribute to Subjective Well-being?" no. 332. https://doi.org/https://doi.org/https:// doi.org/10.1787/5jlz3k7pqc5j-en.

Kuitto, Kati. 2016. "From Social Security to Social Investment? Compensating and Social Investment Welfare Policies in a Life-Course Perspective." *Journal of European Social Policy* 26 (5): 442–59.

Leoni, Thomas. 2016. "Social Investment as a Perspective on Welfare State Transformation in Europe." *Intereconomics* 51 (4). https://doi.org/10.1007/s10272 -016-0601-3.

Mazzucato, Mariana. 2013. *The Entrepreneurial State: Debunking Public vs. Private Sector Myths.* New York: Anthem Press.

Midgley, J., E. Dahl, and A. Wright (eds). 2017. *Social Investment and Social Welfare. International and Critical Perspectives.* Cheltenham, UK and Northampton, MA, USA: Edward Elgar Publishing.

Morel, N., B. Palier, and J. Palme (eds). 2012. *Towards a Social Investment Welfare State? Ideas, Policies and Challenges.* Bristol: Policy Press.

Neimanns, Erik, Marius R. Busemeyer, and Julian L. Garritzmann. 2018. "How Popular Are Social Investment Policies Really? Evidence from a Survey Experiment in Eight Western European Countries." *European Sociological Review.* https://doi .org/10.1093/esr/jcy008.

Nolan, Brian. 2013. "What Use Is 'Social Investment'?" *Journal of European Social Policy* 23 (5): 459–68.

Parolin, Zachary, and Wim Van Lancker. 2021. "What a Social Investment 'Litmus Test' Must Address: A Response to Plavgo and Hemerijck." *Journal of European Social Policy* 31 (3): 297–308.

Plavgo, Ilze, and Anton Hemerijck. 2020. "The Social Investment Litmus Test: Family Formation, Employment and Poverty." *Journal of European Social Policy*, 0958928720950627.

Ronchi, Stefano. 2016. "The Social Investment Welfare Expenditure Data Set (SIWE)." GK SOCLIFE Working Paper.

Ronchi, Stefano. 2018. "Which Roads (If Any) to Social Investment? The Recalibration of EU Welfare States at the Crisis Crossroads (2000–2014)." *Journal of Social Policy* 47 (3): 459–78. https://doi.org/10.1017/S0047279417000782.

Sakamoto, Takayuki. 2021. "Do Social Investment Policies Reduce Income Inequality? An Analysis of Industrial Countries." *Journal of European Social Policy* 31 (4): 440–56.

Sen, Amartya. 2006. "The Capability Approach in Development." *The Journal of Political Philosophy*. https://doi.org/10.1111/j.1467-9760.2006.00263.x.

Sen, Amartya. 2008. "The Economics of Happiness and Capability." In *Capabilities and Happiness*, edited by Luigino Bruni, Flavio Comim, and Maurizio Pugno, 16–27. Oxford: Oxford University Press.

12. Challenges for the public sector – a few concluding remarks

12.1 INTRODUCTION

Most countries have faced, and can be expected to face in the future, a number of challenges for the public sector. There will probably be constant challenges for the public sector as a result of changes in the way society functions, changing preferences of citizens, globalization and new technological opportunities. Therefore, the following should be seen as an indication of some key challenges that are known at present. They do not have to be the same in all countries and at all times due to historical differences and traditions. The challenges of globalization are dealt with in Chapter 10.

This last chapter presents a number of the challenges facing the public sector in both the short and long term. A key challenge is the demographic development with an ageing population, which will put pressure on, in particular, spending in relation to elderly care and healthcare, which is discussed in Section 12.2.

It is also important to have an idea about how the public sector can be better prepared for international crises, such as the financial crisis and the recent COVID-19 crisis, as this might require a longer time horizon in planning and to ensure an economic buffer. This is the focus in Section 12.3.

Technological developments will also challenge the public sector in terms of both expenditure and revenue. This is discussed in Section 12.4. Lastly, in Section 12.5, the chapter discusses the legitimacy of the public sector and how this might influence public sector economy. Section 12.6 concludes the chapter.

12.2 DEMOGRAPHIC CHALLENGES

The composition of the population has changed and is expected to continue to change. This is shown in Figure 12.1 for the EU for the time until 2100.

Figure 12.1 clearly shows that there will be a marked growth of people aged over 65, and especially the proportion of people aged 80 and over will be growing so that in the year 2100 they will amount to approximately every

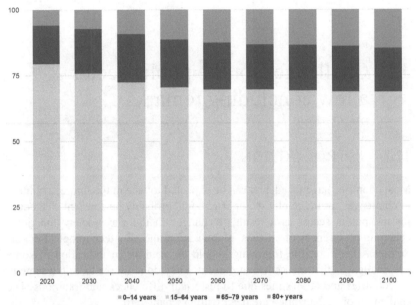

Note: 2020: provisional; 2030–2100: projections (EUROPOP2019).
Source: https://ec.europa.eu/eurostat/statistics-explained/index.php?title=Population_structure
_and_ageing#The_share_of_elderly_people_continues_to_increase, accessed 25 November
2021.

*Figure 12.1   Population structure by major age groups, EU, 2020–2100
                (% of total population)*

seventh person in the population, and almost every third person will be over
65 years old. During the same period, there will be no changes in the share
of children and young people in the population. There will be differences in
the size of the changes across developed countries, but there will be strong
changes overall, although not in exactly the same years for all.

The demographic changes have some potential consequences for the public
sector economy. Firstly, if the same level of service is to be maintained, more
resources will be needed in the area of health and care for elderly, and if no
more taxes and duties are decided, or there is a real growth in the economies,
this money, if any, will have to come from other areas of the public sector
economy. This also exemplifies the possible cross-pressure across the public
sector's activities in the coming years.

Secondly, that there may be a risk that there will be a shortage of labour as
there will be a declining proportion of the population who are of working age.
This can be seen from the development of the dependency ratio. As can be seen
in Table 12.1, it will be significantly changed. The old-age dependency ratio

Table 12.1   Old-age dependency ratio from 2020 to 2100

	2020	2030	2040	2050	2060	2070	2080	2090	2100
Dependency ratio (%)	31.8	39.2	46.7	51.9	54.0	54.0	55.7	56.8	57.1

Source: See Figure 12.1.

is defined as the +65-year-old/15–64-year-old. Although it can be discussed whether the boundaries should just be in these years, it is in any case an indication of the extent of change.

Table 12.1 shows that especially until the year 2050 there will be strong changes influencing the spending needs, but also a gradual change after that because the fertility rate in all European countries is below the reproduction rate.

Thirdly, if people in retirement (the retirement age can, of course, be raised) have no other income, there may be a pressure on public revenues depending on the structure of the pension system (as described in Chapter 9) as more people will be eligible to receive old-age pension.

There are a number of elements that can dampen the demographic pressure on the public sector economy.

Firstly, not only do we live longer, but we also have more healthy life years in which there is less need for care and attention. Better health might also imply that more people stay on the labour market longer than today, and this will also reduce the financial burden on the public sector.

Secondly, there will be welfare technology that can relieve the need for personal help, and thus further reduce the risk of labour shortages in the health and care areas.

So it can be discussed whether there is a time-bomb on the way, as also pointed out a long time ago (Greve 2006).

However, a change in age composition is not the only element that affects development. In a number of countries, there is also the tendency for more people to live alone, which, for example, for single parents can increase the need for help in caring for children, and for the elderly, help to avoid feeling lonely.

12.3   HOW TO PREPARE FOR FUTURE EXTERNAL SHOCKS?

As already pointed out earlier in the book, one possibility for being prepared for future economic shocks will be that there is room to change public spending to enable, for example, people to keep their jobs as a result of a new crisis. As a result, government debt must avoid becoming excessive, just as large yearly government deficits can be problematic. The risk of large debts is, in other words, that interest expenses on the debt can act as a deterrent to incurring expenses, including those that can be seen as an investment in the future, for example.

It must, of course, be balanced after investing in the future as well, for example, in infrastructure such as roads, public transport, airports, IT, and so on. There will therefore also be a need to try to estimate the long-term economic development in order to be able to balance wishes and expectations in a large number of areas, and here (as described earlier in the book) cost-benefit and cost-effectiveness analysis of some instruments may be used to make such assessments.

This can also include investment in education to ensure that the labour force has the necessary competences for the possible new types of jobs. Investing in order to ensure sustainability, for example, to reduce the risk of flooding in some countries, or other ways to reduce CO_2 emissions is also important.

Thus, part of how to prepare for the future might involve a combination of sound economic steering with investment in the future, including preparations for those changes that we already know about and which, presumably, will actually take place.

12.4   TECHNOLOGY AND THE PUBLIC SECTOR

The technological development not only contributes to richer societies, which can also solve a number of problems, including for example in the environmental field, but can also contribute to a number of challenges for the public sector in a number of ways.

Firstly, we have seen tendencies that technology in a number of areas has contributed to monopoly or monopoly-like development, where as a result of market power there is also a greater degree of inequality with a few who have very large incomes and fortunes (Antonin et al. 2020; Eeckhout 2020; Aghion, Antonin, and Bunel 2021).

Secondly, new technology means that there may be pressure on public spending, for example, to be able to use the latest technology in the field of health sector to help people with the best possible treatment. New technology can also make certain activities (including in the field of health sector) cheaper, by enabling more decentralized support, better medicine and earlier knowledge about the need for treatment.

Thirdly, there is a risk that a large number of jobs will become redundant. Up to 50 per cent of all job functions are at risk of disappearing or being drastically changed. The technological development thus risks making many unemployed either permanently or for a shorter period of time. It will make demands on education and labour market policy if this is to be reduced, including that people have the skills that will be necessary to be able to get the new jobs that are also created by new technology (Arntz, Gregory, and Zierahn 2017; OECD 2019; Georgieff and Milanez 2021).

Fourthly, new technology could contribute to higher productivity in the public sector, both through the administration of, for example, income transfers and the production of certain services, for example, in the health sector. The calculation of productivity can be difficult within the public sector as a result of the way in which the value of public sector production is calculated, but there may be ways to measure it. The number of operations with a given input of labour can, for example, be expected to increase as new technology becomes possible. The collection and securing of the necessary taxation can also be facilitated.

Fifthly, new technology, both as a result of changes in the labour market and also capital movements, can make it more difficult to know where companies have their activities and thus where they are to be taxed (cf. also Chapter 6 for a discussion on this).

Overall, new technology offers a number of opportunities for good economic development, but it can have a number of secondary effects in relation to distribution, use of labour, and so on, which poses challenges for the public sector economy. This also includes a possible need for transferring resources from areas with fewer persons to areas with a growing need for public support.

12.5   LEGITIMACY AND THE PUBLIC SECTOR

The tasks of the public sector, such as providing public goods and reducing market failures, do not in themselves say anything about the scope and size of the public sector to solve these problems. In addition, tasks related to distribution will be influenced by normative attitudes to how much inequality both currently and over a life-course can be accepted. It can also influence attitudes towards which instruments to choose, including how sustainable economic and environmental development can be ensured.

Consequently, it will also be important to know the extent to which the activities and decisions of the public sector are seen as legitimate by the population of a country. This is also due to the fact that although there are good arguments, for example, that there is a joint responsibility for long-term care, if everyone either has to take out insurance or save up to cover any expenses for this, it will not be economically optimal.

Similarly, the size of the coverage and replacement ratio will depend not only on an assessment of how it affects incentives to work, but also whether there is support in the population to pay for it and the level of this support . It might even be the case that there is support for some types of benefits, such as pensions, but not necessarily for benefits to the unemployed.

Legitimacy can be influenced by populist views, including welfare chauvinism, but also by whether the public sector is seen as effective in solving its tasks. Both can affect, for example, the willingness to pay the necessary taxes and fees to finance public sector activities (Greve 2019).

This also illustrates a need for a reconciliation of expectations in relation to the coverage of both service and income transfers in relation to the electorate, and what it is possible to finance in the coming years.

12.6 CONCLUDING REMARKS

The public sector plays a key role in all modern societies in helping to ensure the best possible use of scarce resources. The public sector also ensures the provision of public goods such as the judiciary, legislation, police and foreign services. In addition, the development of infrastructure is an important task. Similarly, the possibility of influencing the allocation, distribution and stabilization of societal economic development.

The extent to which the distribution over the life-course as well as in individual years should be affected is ultimately a political problem. However, knowledge of the consequences of various forms of intervention in the social economy for not only the distribution, but also the overall economic activity and employment can be important elements to be aware of.

This also applies to the short- and long-term consequences of activities, including social investment, and how the public sector can contribute to strengthening the development of the private sector, and not be a burden to the private sector. The necessary interplay between public and private activity and interdependence can be better understood when looking precisely at how the public sector in a number of areas, such as education and infrastructure, supports the development of the private sector, while the private sector through production and employment contributes to the economic financing of the public sector. There might also be a need for rethinking the welfare state more broadly (Greve 2022).

Overall, the book hopefully contributed to a clarification of a number of the roles and tasks that the public sector can carry out, and how it is possible to assess the consequences of this.

REFERENCES

Aghion, Philippe, Céline Antonin, and Simon Bunel. 2021. *The Power of Creative Destruction.* Cambridge, MA: Harvard University Press.
Antonin, Céline, Simon Bunel, Xavier Jaravel, and Philippe Aghion. 2020. "What Are the Labor and Product Market Effects of Automation? New Evidence from France." Paris. https://www.college-de-france.fr/media/philippe-aghion/UPL669053661 1808175234_aabj_jan5.pdf, accessed 10 January 2022.

Arntz, Melanie, Terry Gregory, and Ulrich Zierahn. 2017. "Revisiting the Risk of Automation." *Economics Letters*. https://doi.org/10.1016/j.econlet.2017.07.001.

Eeckhout, Jan. 2020. *The Profit Paradox*, 1st edn, 327. Princeton, NJ: Princeton University Press.

Georgieff, Alexandre, and Anna Milanez. 2021. "What Happened to Jobs at High Risk of Automation?" 255. OECD Social, Employment and Migration Working Papers. Paris: OECD.

Greve, B. 2006. "Is There a Demographic Time-Bomb?" In *The Future of the Welfare State. European and Global Perspectives*, edited by B. Greve, 1st edn, 27–36. Hampshire: Ashgate.

Greve, B. 2019. *Welfare, Populism and Welfare Chauvinism*. Bristol: Policy Press.

Greve, B. 2022. *Rethinking the Welfare State*. Cheltenham, UK and Northampton, MA, USA: Edward Elgar Publishing.

OECD. 2019. *OECD Employment Outlook 2019: The Future of Work*. Paris: OECD.

Index